MAYAN HORROR

REVIEWS OF MAYAN HORROR

"Twice as funny as…anything written…by Peter C. Newman."
—Yeuda Mann, *Markham Weekly Auto Trader*

"If you only read one book between now and December 21st, 2012, you are a very slow reader."
—Orlando Curtainbach, *I Love Toronto Quarterly*

"A refreshing change of pace from his earlier novels about Serbian welders, this book fairly dances along at a pace that keeps the reader quickly turning the page while, at the same time, looking forward to turning the next page."
—Richard Trickle, *Sparwood Weekly Sheet*

"*Mayan Horror*…not only explains what might happen when the Mayan Calendar ends but…is so good that…you start salivating at the thought of being consumed by a giant ball of fire, or eaten alive by swarms of gnats, or even flattened by a falling Winnebago."
—Lana Lovely, *Parliament Hill Bus Schedule*

"A book of incredible emotional wisdom with characters that literally jump off the page…is what I'm currently reading and, very soon, I will get around to reading Mr. Robertson's book."
—Esther Skidmore, *North Flin Flon Women's Reading Club*

MAYAN HORROR

How to Survive the End of the World in 2012

BOB ROBERTSON

Anvil Press • Vancouver • 2011

Copyright © 2011 by Bob Robertson

Anvil Press Publishers Inc.
P.O. Box 3008, Main Post Office
Vancouver, B.C. V6B 3X5 Canada
www.anvilpress.com

All rights reserved. No part of this book may be reproduced by any means without the prior written permission of the publisher, with the exception of brief passages in reviews. Any request for photocopying or other reprographic copying of any part of this book must be directed in writing to ACCESS: The Canadian Copyright Licensing Agency, One Yonge Street, Suite 800, Toronto, Ontario, Canada, M5E 1E5.

Library and Archives Canada Cataloguing in Publication

Robertson, Bob
    Mayan horror : how to survive the end of the world in 2012 / Bob Robertson.

ISBN 978-1-897535-87-5
1. Maya calendar—Miscellanea.
2. End of the world—Humor. I. Title.

F1435.3.C14R63 2011   001.902'07   C2011-906154-6

Printed and bound in Canada
Cover design: Rayola.com
Interior design: Heimat House
Illustrations: Mark Pilon

Represented in Canada by the Literary Press Group

Distributed in Canada by the University of Toronto Press and in the U.S. by Small Press Distribution (SPD).

The publisher gratefully acknowledges the financial assistance of the Canada Council for the Arts, the Canda Book Fund, and the Province of British Columbia through the B.C. Arts Council and the Book Publishing Tax Credit.

"To Linda
'til Mayans do us part"

Table of Contents

Foreword • 9

1) No Christians Allowed • 13
2) Who The Heck Are The Mayans And What's With Their Calendar? • 23
3) Possible World Endings And How To Survive Them • 33
4) It's Gone? The Hell, You Say! • 55
5) Heaven, I'm In Heaven • 63
6) How To Talk To Your Children About The Annihilation Of Earth • 73
7) Bearers Of Bad Tidings (EAS) • 81
8) The Ten Safest Places In Canada To Wait Out The Apocalypse • 91
9) The Countdown • 103
10) How To Build Your Own Government And Get It Right This Time • 109
11) Excellent Business Opportunities After Doomsday • 119
12) Questions From Frightened Readers • 127
13) Mayan Horror Readers Book Club • 139

Mayan Horror Index • 141
Other Books by Bob Robertson • 152
Acknowledgements • 155
About the Author • 158

Foreword

Let me introduce myself. I am Professor A. Jinkerson, PVC, MLB, DsT. I was very pleased to be asked to write the foreword to this landmark book. As a trained catastrophysicist and the lead scientist at the Armageddon Lab here at the University of Southern British Columbia, I have dedicated my entire professional life to searching for a cure for cataclysms. Although we have not achieved that breakthrough yet, we have made some exciting discoveries. One of our discoveries is that the "annihilation" of the world is eminently survivable if you have been suitably forewarned and forearmed, and given the tools to ride out the conflagration. This is why the book you are holding in your hands is so valuable.

The author, Bob Robertson, and I are completely in sync on this one important point: just because the oceans are rising up, the earth's tectonic plates are wrenched apart, and molten lava rains down from the sky, doesn't mean you can't come out smiling on the other end. Bob's uncanny ability to clearly explain cataclysmic events was first evident in his groundbreaking children's book on the Big Bang, titled *What if God Lit His Fart?* He followed that up with an enlightening book about the Great Flood called *How Did Noah Round Up Two Fruit Flies?* His award-winning documentary about Pompeii, *Running Quickly in Sandals*, won the Caligula Prize for Pallid Writing at the Win By Luck Festival in Come By Chance, Newfoundland. Now this book, *Mayan Horror: How to Survive the End of the World in 2012*, picks up where his last book, *The Aztecs Predicted George W. Bush*, left off.

Here on the rambling USBC campus, with its commanding views of the iconic Pitt Meadows skyline, we have worked steadily to decipher the Mesoamerican Long Count Calendar, the very instrument that will bring about the destruction of the earth on December 21st, 2012. One great question remains unanswered: what kind of End Time event will actually happen when the Mayan Calendar stops? Bob Robertson has covered all the possible scenarios that a planet-ending catastrophe could bring to humanity, from the ubiquitous (monster earthquakes) to the more obscure (downpour of frogs and salamanders). His painstaking research will guide you through each possible crisis and offer some helpful tips for avoiding painful death, dismemberment, and even embarrassment over poor wardrobe choices.

But this book is more than simply a guide to surviving the apocalypse. You will also find chapters to help you prosper in a post-apocalyptic world, with tips on how to become wealthy overnight by cornering the market on much-needed products in a devastated landscape. The book also shows you how to start a government from scratch and how to avoid common pitfalls, like ending up with a right wing, micro-managing megalomaniac as leader. It's all here. As I write this now, our team is working on a wind-tunnel simulation of the "outbreak of boils" scenario. Anything is possible once that Mayan calendar stops.

I'll leave you with this thought: here on our Pitt Meadows campus, I double as both the lead scientist at the Armageddon Lab and head coach of our football team, the Pitts. As such, I have to deal with both the long count and the short snap. Get caught off guard with either and you will have a serious protection breakdown, a mess in your backfield, and, ultimately, you will be sacked. Read this book. It just might save your life.

Believing that sunglasses would protect them from any disaster, the Wirral Sisters decided to sit back, relax, and let the Mayan Calendar do its worst.

1.

No Christians Allowed

Before we get started on who the Mayans are and what will happen when their infamous calendar screeches to a stop on December 21st, 2012, let me emphatically state: Christians should keep their big holy noses out of this. No matter what gobbledygook they spout, I can assure you that this is not their long-awaited Judgment Day (or any other religion's judgment day for that matter, it's just that Christians go on about it so much more than the others do because they have a warped obsession over the return of their Lord and Saviour). The evangelicals don't like to hear this, but if space aliens landed on earth today, they would quickly come to the conclusion that Jesus Christ is, in fact, the god of traffic jams, based on how many times his name is screamed out during those occurrences. They'd probably also come to the conclusion that Asshole is the god of car drivers being cut off, based on how many times His name is screamed out during those moments.

We'll deal more with "Asshole" shortly, when we get to Pastor Harold Camping, but in the meantime, let's talk about this Christian obsession with the flaming return of Jesus, the man/god they are so desperate to have back so he can snatch the true believers out of harm's way and leave the rest of the humans to die painful deaths. For our non-Christian readers not familiar with all this, here's the backstory. Once upon a time, according to religious texts, God and the Holy Ghost had a pretty good partnership going running the universe. God was more the CEO, making major policy decisions. The Holy Ghost handled the human resources side of things, trying to figure out why human beings acted so strangely—so, mostly, he just did a lot of shrugging at directors' meetings. One day, God decided they needed a third partner, and He thought they should bring in a human and create an HR department. Plus, He had a hankering for a son who could carry on the family business after He had died.

But God didn't want to take his chances and let two humans mate, in case He ended up with a kid with ADHD who wet the bed and had screaming fits while they were out shopping. Worse yet, in letting two humans mate you might actually end up with a girl, and "The Daughter of God" would just not go down well on a macho planet like Earth. To guarantee that He got a boy and that the kid was healthy, the third partner in the Universe needed to be half-human, half-god. That meant God had to send the Holy Ghost out on an insemination run, and do it without anyone knowing about it.

That part was pretty easy, because he was an invisible ghost and could slip in and out unseen, if you know what I mean. The plan worked pretty well, although, in His mad rush to have a child, God didn't take into consideration the fact that Joseph, the husband of the lucky girl impregnated, would be laughed at down at his local oasis watering hole because he had to tell the guys that an invisible man got his wife pregnant.

Anyway, when all was said and done, God had two babies, both boys. Jesus was the older of the two. The younger of God's two sons was Mohammed, who had a mysterious beginning to his life. He was an orphan so no one knew who his parents were, but of course it's pretty obvious to us that it was the Holy Ghost on another of his crazy shagging weekends in town. Interestingly, God didn't know about that one, making Mohammed the Oops Baby, the one who caught God by surprise. Having a brother who was 570 years older meant Mohammed usually ended up playing by himself and with a dad who was very elderly—like about thirteen billion years old—and there was little chance of him throwing the football around with Mohammed. As a result, Christians have had very little interest in the younger of God's two children, which is typical in most families where the oldest, the "Golden Boy," gets all the attention.

Most of you know the story of Jesus's life. He died young, and ever since then Christians have been fixated on having him come back to earth, guns blazing, to load up his spaceship only with people who have the special wristbands. That's why, over the last two thousand years, Christians have continued to predict various dates for his second coming, but, with a zero per cent success rate, they have done really poorly. In fact, in the "Guessing the date of the Rapture" department, Christians are the most useless of all, even worse than Nostradamus who called for the world to end in July 1999. Yes, the legendary Nostradamus! How could a man who predicted Brad and Jenn's breakup to the exact day be so wrong about the end of the world? So, the Christians are not alone in their totally inaccurate annihilation dates. However, they are relentless in their panicky announcements of when Jesus will land and start the roundup.

There are hundreds of examples of erroneous Christian predictions. There was Hilary of Poitiers, who called for the world to end in the year 367 and got it wrong, but then why would you believe a man named Hilary? There was the Spanish monk who suddenly blurted out into a crowded marketplace that the world would end that night. Well, it didn't, and the guys in charge of his monastery decided it would be best if he didn't spend so much time in the Benedictine tasting room. Then there was great distress in 999, as the year 1000 drew near, with Christians figuring that was when life on earth would end—sort of a Y1K panic. I guess they thought their abacuses couldn't handle a year with four numbers in it instead of three. Same result. The conflagration was a no-show. Which brings me to the year 2011 and the antics of Christianity's "Buffoon of the Year" trophy winner, the radio evangelist Harold Camping. I would call him an idiot, but that would give idiots a bad name, and he has already given camping a bad name. Harold is the president of "Family Radio," which is dedicated to getting families to sell their homes and cars and to cash in their savings so that Harold can buy hundreds of giant billboards announcing the end of the world on May 21st. "Oops! Sorry folks. I meant to say October 21st. Oops! What I meant to say was, ah, we take MasterCard and VISA!" If that's radio for the family, I think Manson Family Radio might be more palatable.

So, yet another Christian gets Armageddon dates wrong. Compare that to the Mayans. Only once in their three-thousand-year history, did they signal the end of everything through their amazing calendar. Their calculations are totally scientific, worked out thousands of years ago using astronomical measurements and algorithms so that December 21st, 2012 is represented on the Mayan calendar as 13.0.0.0.0. How ingenious is that? Harold "Bad Math" Camping, on the other hand, worked out his various world-ending dates using this formula. Let me quote Pastor Camping from his radio program:

> "Friends, the Bible constantly talks about the Rapture and all the means of death that will come from it, if ye are not amongst those who faithfully contribute to our program. 'And the flames of the Lord will lick at your tender parts and when the licking has ended, ye will be well-licked and death shall be upon thee like a tree falling in the forest, which everyone will hear,

Condiments four, verses six and seven: 'And slimy antlers will grow within your pajama bottoms and rip apart your loins, severing a major artery and bleeding you to death in less than four minutes,' Saint Buffy-Marie, chapter nine, verse three. 'If ye of little faith will only subscribe, ye will be free of rattlesnakes squeezing your testicles until they swell up and explode in a spray of broken blood vessels and tiny skin fragments,' Rotarians seventeen, verse eleven. Listen to this, from Gloccamora three, verses eight and nine: 'And when the end comes, ye will know because the mucous membranes inside your nose will peel off and slide down your throat causing great heaving, and fluid evacuation.'

Or, these words, 'Yea, will scaly scabs form on your armpits and incubate giant lice which will burrow into the skin of your lower limbs,' GlenLivet eighteen, verse seven. And worst of all, friends, 'Those who have not sent money to this program will be set upon by a plague of maggots, wriggling and slimy, which will nest in the orifices of their body and multiply daily by the thousands until becoming dung beetles and living off thy daily sphincter squeezings, and all will occur on the twenty-first of the fifth month in the year of our Lord, 2011.' Gigabytes twenty-three, verse sixteen. Please remember, friends, that if you do not want to die in that apocalypse with bats flying out your butt, send money now to our program.

"Cash in your life savings, everything you've got, empty your children's piggy banks, go through grandma's purse. But if ye fail to do so, friends, when that great day of reckoning comes on the date named in Gigabytes twenty-three, verse sixteen, then heed the warnings from the Epistle to the Listerines, chapter twelve, verse fourteen, 'For when the Apocalypse shall descend over you, unless ye have contributed mightily to the ministry of Pastor Harold Camping, ye shall be tied under a camel's hind legs during mating season and be forced to sing "Feelings" over and over.' God bless, friends. Please remember that Jesus is coming on May 21st, but if he does not show his heavenly face that day, there are so many other days and months and years that he can choose from and we will keep you posted through our giant, nation-wide, listener-supported billboards when we receive an updated schedule from the word of God. In the meantime, keep that money pouring in."

That was Pastor Camping trying to frighten you into liquidating your assets and investing in highway billboards. Listen up, Christians! This end-of-the-world cataclysm has nothing to do with you. The Mayans thought up the end of the calendar in 2012, thousands of years before there even were Christians. It's time to let the Mayans see if they can get one right, so stay the hell out of this, Harold Camping! Get your own damned apocalypse!

And if Christians needed another good reason why Jesus won't be coming back on December 21st, it's pretty obvious.

It's winter in the northern hemisphere, the shortest day of the year—there could be blizzard warnings and temperatures so cold your tongue will freeze just thinking about licking a lamp post. So, Jesus would have to go around in a parka hammering his mittens on doors saying, "Hi, we're in your neighbourhood looking for people who believe in me. If you do, just sign here. You'll get a free trip to heaven plus accommodation for eternity, plus we take Air Miles. If you do not sign up, you will be left behind to die a ghastly death and then probably be eaten by packs of wild dogs. Okay?" No, Jesus wouldn't come back during the Canadian winter, especially once hockey season is in full swing. He'd have to hope he could get a mention from Don Cherry on *Coach's Corner*, and that's not likely because Don Cherry hates foreigners, especially if they have long hair.

Points to Ponder from the chapter "No Christians Allowed"

What constitutes a true Christian? This is important if you still believe that Jesus is coming in December 2012. For example, I was baptized a Christian, and thinking back on the words in that service, which is rare for a three-month-old baby to be able to remember, that should have given me the special wristband I mentioned in the chapter to signal to Jesus during the Rapture that I have a reserved seat on his heaven-bound craft. The minister said, and I don't remember everything from the service because I was screaming loudly after pooping my diaper, "This child is saved! His sins have been washed away." But consider this: many years later I received my confirmation in a separate service where I was supposed to have studied in order to be officially confirmed. Well, I didn't study, I fooled around in the basement all night with my hockey stick, shooting a tennis ball against the wall pretending I was Gordie Howe, and then I lied to get that confirmation certificate. Those aren't the actions of a true Christian, are they? So, you see, I feel good about what'll happen to me during the Mayan conflagration, but if it's the Rapture, I think I'll get left behind with all the riff-raff. How about you?

As his favourite clock ticked down to the end of the world, Stan decided to go out with a smile on his face, holding on to what he loved most in life: his first place trophies in the annual pie eating contest and the lucky utensils that brought him victory.

2.

Who The Heck Are The Mayans And What's With Their Calendar?

Up 'til about two years ago you would never have heard any mention of the Mayans, unless you took a day trip from your Cancun beach holiday to visit "The Ruins" and, even then, most people would pull the old "Jump from the bus, stand in front of the temple, snap the photo, back on the bus 'cause it's almost Happy Hour at Carlos 'n' Charlie's." Or maybe your favourite TV channel was National Geographic, especially when they ran those Mesoamerican Marathons. So you've gone from Mayans rarely ever being mentioned to "All Mayans All the Time." You can't read a newspaper or turn on your TV without Mayans being mentioned, like these recent headlines: "Mayans believed responsible for Global Warming," "Vancouver Canucks Trade Luongo for Two Mayans," or, in the *National Enquirer*, "Oprah balloons up to 400 pounds in preparation for Mayan apocalypse." Even on the front of the *Weekly World News*: "Bat Boy to lead first wave of Mayan attackers on December 21st." And TV's *Entertainment Tonight*, having milked Michael Jackson, Mel Gibson, Charlie Sheen and Arnold Schwarzenegger stories dry, has turned to the Mayan Horror. Just last night, the hosts were yelling, "And wait 'til you see which of the Kardashian sisters has been dating a Mayan!" Yes, now people can't shut up about the Mayans, the ancient race that created a calendar, which was a pretty handy thing for three or four thousand years, letting the Mayans keep medicine man appointments or reminding them when to grind the maize, and yet comes to a mysterious screeching stop on December 21st, 2012.

Now the whole world is forced to prepare for whatever horrific events will happen when the calendar strikes 11:11 a.m. Universal Time (This used to be Greenwich Mean Time but somebody thought Greenwich was getting way too much publicity). So, how is it possible that people believe the world will end thanks to the Mayans, but they don't even know the first thing about this ancient race? That's because high schools have stopped teaching history and replaced it with dodge-ball lessons or Online Gaming 101.

It's time to find out who the Mayans are and why they are bringing rack and ruin to the earth. Okay, I exaggerate. There is no mention of them bringing rack, just ruin. I was just hoping there might be some rack first and that would give us time to get ready for the ruin which always follows just after the rack, but it was simply wishful thinking on my part. So, a lack of rack but plenty of ruin coming our way.

Let's start with who the Mayans are. Although there are plenty of ordinary Mayans still around today, the ones who designed this killer calendar were one of the world's super races at a time when super races were all the rage. Everybody had to have a super race. You had the Egyptians, the Aztecs, the Greeks, the Atlantians, even the Lemurians who, I gather, were lemurs but they could levitate and often travelled to Uranus and back just to pick berries. Every one of those super races disappeared and nothing like them has ever been seen again. Yes, I know Hitler tried to create a super race of Aryans, but all he got was a stadium full of pasty-faced assholes with a superiority complex who could only raise one arm. Hitler didn't create a super race; he created a stupor race.

So let's start with where this super race of Mayans came from. The Mayan civilization existed in what is now Central America and Mexico at a time when you could actually drink the water down there and didn't have to brush your teeth with Corona, a time when Montezuma's Revenge meant only a massive attack by hundreds of warriors who came to hack off heads, not a loosening of the bowels. The Mayans seemed to especially like the Yucatan Peninsula, which, nowadays, is one of the states of Mexico but back then it was called "Yokatlan" which means "place of richness." Sadly, all you had to do was say the word "richness" to the plundering Spanish conquistadors and the fine hairs on their testicles stood on end as they envisioned mountains of gold, and dreamed of returning to Spain with so much bling around their necks, they would be swarmed by women wanting to rip off their doublets and hose and curly-toed shoes and fondle their bangles.

But before Pizarro, Balboa, Ponce de Leon and their Spanish brothers-in-tights arrived and started sticking their flags into things, the Mayan super race owned the Yucatan. The people who have now sealed our doom with their cunning calendar were quite brilliant. Not as smart as Ken Jennings, the Jeopardy multi-millionaire ("I'll take Quantum Electrodynamic Theory for two hundred, Alex"), but they were really smart. The Mayans were very accomplished astronomers and mathematicians, thousands of years ahead of their time. Now, they also believed that the earth was flat, but I figure two out of three ain't bad. How the Mayans got to be such whizzes at astronomy is a mystery considering they had their super race going full swing way back in 3000 BC, and every Mayan youngster could recite all the details of the Zenial Passages of the Sun. Over five thousand years later, it's hard to find a teenager who can even tell you where the sun is because that would mean having to look up from his iPhone.

One theory on why the Mayans were such geniuses came from a Swiss writer named Erich von Däniken who wrote a book called *Chariots of the Gods?*, wherein he claimed that all these super races got to be that smart because aliens came down to earth in flying saucers and taught them things like math and astronomy. Remember that book? Those were the seventies, when people were easily sucked into believing all sorts of loony things, like flying saucers landing on earth, or that little rocks could actually be pets. I have a serious problem with von Däniken's theory because if the tiny bug-eyed spacemen taught all these super races things like astronomy and mathematics, why did they stop there? Why couldn't they have taught humans other important things like the difference between "All you can eat" and "All you should eat"? Wouldn't that alone have made the world a better place to live in?

Aliens coming to earth is a little hard for me to believe. Having said that, maybe von Däniken was right, because how else could the Mayans have built the massive temple at Chichen Itza without the use of alien space tools like a 2.2 Tonne Anti-gravity Vibratory Pile Driver or a Thought-Activated Articulating Boom Forklift? Okay, yes, I admit, it is possible that they built those temples by whipping thousands of slaves 'til they bled, making them pull ropes and haul fifty-tonne stones seventy-five feet in the air, but, you have to admit that alien space tools sounds like a much more practical way to build these pyramids.

And another thing that von Däniken didn't mention in his theory of slimy little ETs teaching the Mayans how to be a super race: anal probing. These days the Internet and all-night radio shows are buzzing with stories of alien abductions and, in every one of the statements to police, the abductees say the only thing the aliens wanted was to stick a probe in their anuses. Like you, I'm a little disappointed that advanced races of beings would travel three hundred light years just to inspect human bums. Perhaps, between then and now, there's been a change of focus on alien planets, away from teaching science and math to some kind of porn fetish. Who knows, maybe they eat humans and it is not an anal probe at all, but merely a meat thermometer sticking out of the abductee's back passage. But, I digress. Whether you believe it was through alien intervention or not, there's no doubt that the Mayans were a super race way ahead of today's modern humans.

Besides astronomy and math, the Mayans invented a ball game, which they cleverly called "ballgame." Ballgame was played in an arena in front of thousands of screaming fans, some chanting, some singing "You'll Never Walk Alone." Instead of cheerleaders at the end of the second quarter, the half-time shows featured, and I'm not kidding, human sacrifices. The announcer would say something like, "Ladies and Gentlemen, it's time for tonight's human sacrifice. Check page thirty-four of your ballgame program for your seat and row number. The lucky victim of the human sacrifice tonight is in row twenty-four, seat B21. Come on down!" The Mayans also perfected the blowgun that used poisonous darts. If you closely inspect the figures on the sides of Mayan temple walls, there is one figure that appears to be slumped on the ground underneath the message, "Never suck on a blowgun!" Archeologists have no idea how many blowguns the Mayans had at any one time. Unlike Canada, I'm sure the Mayans didn't have a blowgun registry, but I'll bet every Mayan kept a blowgun under his pillow just in case there was a sneak attack by Toltecs in the middle of the night, or in case an Inca broke into their hut and tried to make off with their statue of Itzpapalotl. The Mayans also invented musical instruments like the iconic pan-pipes, which, thousand of years later, migrated north from the Yucatan and can now be heard on the street corners of every major Canadian city.

Long before fat people were shoving candy bars into their mouths, the Mayans invented chocolate, or, as it was called back then, cacao. The name was changed to chocolate in modern times because people found they couldn't enjoy a snack that had the word "caca" in it, and yet, it's odd isn't it, they still happily munch on pistachios. Cacao was not only a bean the Mayans used for making drinks and food, but cacao beans were so valuable, they were used as currency, so, no doubt, the Mayans invented accountants, or "bean counters" as they would have called them. I wonder if Mayan bean counters had a better sense of humour than ours do? Or did they have accountant jokes too back then, like, "So a bean counter, a high priest and a blowgun shooter are stranded on a desert island…" It probably had a hilarious punch line like "No, said the bean counter, 'debits are on the left, credits are on the right,' at which point the blowgun shooter blew a poisoned dart into his neck and said, 'What do you call a dead bean counter? A good start.'" Here's yet another great invention of the Mayans: horoscopes. When a child was young, the Mayan high priest would come around and give him his own horoscope. "The next six to eight weeks, Micxtlantecihuatxl, will bring new loves/acquaintances into your life, perhaps with that Chichimec girl you had your eye on at the annual Scorpion Festival."

Most importantly, the Mayans invented calendars, and not just the big one that we think will cause all Hell to break loose. The Mayans had a whole bunch of calendars, but the one that concerns us is the calendar the Mayans called "The Long Count Calendar," a calendar that was designed to go for thousands of years. So the question we are all asking ourselves right now is, "Why does this calendar stop at 11:11a.m. Universal Time on December 21st, 2012?" Nobody really knows the answer, but I have a theory: burnout. The guy who chiselled the calendar just got fed up. The chiseller, let's call him Mictxecacihuatxl, was chiseling away on his rock when he just said, "Screw this noise! Do they have any idea how long it takes to chisel ten thousand years worth of dates? And they're only paying me twenty beans a month and all the chimichangas I can eat! Forget it! Maybe it's time to open that dance studio I've fantasized about." And the chiseller downed his tools just after chiseling "12/21/2012" and went off to open "Mictxecacihuatxl's School of Mexican Hat and Chicken Dancing." You may think that sounds like an odd way to condemn the world to ruin, but nobody else seems to have any better ideas as to why the Mayan Calendar stops on December 21st.

One more important thing about the Mayans is that they weren't a monotheistic society, which, for those of you who didn't get past Grade 6, means the Mayans didn't believe there was just one god. The Mayans were a polytheistic society that worshipped all sorts of gods. There was Cizin, the god of death; Chac, the god of rain; Yum Kaax, the god of corn. The list is endless: you've got Discoxxatil, the god of dancing; Xtramunchiz, the god of late night snacks; Maaloxx, the god of upset stomachs; and who could forget Inebriatoxixil, the god of drunks.

You get the point—for everything in ancient Mayan society there was a god you prayed to for more corn, less rain, no hangovers or plenty of chips and salsa. This just reinforces the point that this will not be the Christian God's Armageddon, because in order to make it a godly event, all thirteen hundred of the Mayan gods would have to have gathered together and tried to get an agreement to wipe out the earth. Impossible. I know for example that Shitzaputzl, the god of profanity, would never go along with it. No, we'll have to leave it a mystery as to why the world will end just because the Mayan Calendar runs out, but I'm very fond of the exhausted chiseller theory.

Points to ponder from the chapter "Who The Heck Are The Mayans And What's With Their Calendar?"

I know there are going to be some scholars, and maybe a few modern Mayans, who will disagree with my use of the word "Mayans." They would prefer that everyone use the word "Maya" instead. I am okay with the fact that I will be laughed at by bearded fellows in Tilley hats working at archeological digs from Xlapak all the way down to Yaxchilan. I will survive their snickering and epithets. I'm sticking with "Mayans." What do you think?

3.

Possible World Endings And How To Survive Them

#1. A Mighty Earthquake

This is the gold standard for End of Life fans. What's it like? Typically, after an earthquake, reporters on TV newscasts ask people what it felt like and most of them compare it to a freight train going through their basement. Really? That's what it's comparable to? What the hell kind of houses did they live in where freight trains went through their basement? What did the MLS listing say when they bought the place, "lovely 2 bedroom/1 bathroom bungalow with finished basement complete with freight train tracks"? I have yet to hear anyone say, "Well, it felt like the earth was quaking."

The Mayans were taught astronomy and mathematics by space aliens, such as this one, seen here wearing the futuristic Anti-Matter Binocular Glasses, used for looking at Uranus.

Anyway, let's deal with the "biggest earthquake anyone has ever experienced" suddenly happening on December 21st. Day after day, year after year, people in Vancouver have heard the slogan on their televisions: "Get ready for the Big One." And those are just the Cialis commercials. Seismologists also use the same slogan, just not with the same creepy smiles as worn by the faces of the people in the Cialis commercials.

So, if, at the calendar-ending hour, on a cold winter day, you find yourself looking out the window when the snow lies round about, deep and crisp and even, and you see a poor man gathering fuel, you've suddenly channeled the spirit of Good King Wenceslas. But, if the chandelier starts to sway, dishes and bowling trophies begin toppling off shelves and you think it feels like a freight train is going through your basement, then your first thought should not be, "Did I back up my iTunes downloads?" Your first thought should be to head for cover. You need to stand under something sturdy that won't come down: a doorframe, a desk, or your Google shares.

When all the shaking, swaying and screaming stops, you'll need to get away from your house along with your emergency kit—you know, the one they told everybody to have handy? Right, you forgot. Okay, here's what your emergency earthquake kit should contain: a tent, sleeping bag, camp stove, flashlight, and, most importantly, a copy of *The Boy Scout Campfire Song Book*. This might just save your life on those long, scary nights amidst the post-apocalyptic rubble when nothing will brighten the spirits of earthquake survivors like a few rousing choruses of "Alouette, Gentille Alouette!"

A note to cat owners: after things have settled down, you'll need to find your cats, and, typically, after a massive earthquake you'll usually find them attached to the ceiling, or maybe under the bed. From experience I can assure you they will not be lured off the ceiling using cat treats, I mean, would you? Let's face it, the poor bugger has just seen all nine lives flash in front of his eyes. You will need a sturdy pair of elbow-length welders' gloves to get them down, and, take my word for it again, they will not trust you. In those tiny cat minds, they will believe that you made all that crashing and swinging to punish them for pooping outside their box. Here's a good tip for people who keep more than one cat at home: buy a copy of Lance DeMert's very helpful book, *Herding Cats in an Emergency*. It's a follow-up to his Pulitzer-nominated handbook, *Staging a Goat Rodeo for Fun and Profit*.

Once you and the cats, or even any humans who live with you, get outside your crumbled house, you will notice that your street looks exactly like all the streets in the movie *2012*. The most noticeable difference will be that the acting will be much better on your street. Actually, let's go back to before you left your house, because you are probably looking for tips on what to take with you on your odyssey across a wasted, smoldering landscape. You are officially off the grid now, so anything electronic would be a waste of time. You may encounter flesh-eating zombies on your journey so I would include a bottle of bitter apple spray. I've used it for years to spray the legs of my couch and cats just won't go near it. There's no guarantee it would stop flesh-eating zombies, but it's your best bet, unless you carry one of those knives that Denzel Washington had in *The Book of Eli*, kind of like a two-foot Ginsu knife. That would keep the zombies at bay for a while.

You'll also need something inspiring to read that'll keep your spirits up between leaping twenty-foot cracks in the highway and the rubble from a collapsed IKEA store. Speaking of that, don't take anything from the IKEA store. Trying to assemble furniture from IKEA is a frustrating business at the best of times. After the earthquake you'll have other priorities and you may only have a few weeks to get things done. Also, I suspect Allen keys will be useless in a post-apocalyptic world. This is a fact: U.S. Navy Seals go into precarious situations armed with all the necessary weapons and tools they'll need to survive. Allen keys are not in their arsenal.

Oh, yes, sorry, something inspiring to carry with you to lift your spirits on days when your world just seems to be falling apart, which, of course, it is. I wouldn't bother with a copy of *How to Win Friends and Influence People*, after all, you may never see any people ever again, never mind trying to influence them. Also, you can take a pass on *Awaken the Giant Within*. It turns out that when Tony Robbins was writing it, he was being accused of stealing another man's wife, so I think we know what waking up that giant was all about. Be honest, with most of the planet mangled and smoking, you won't have time for sex or attending Tony Robbins seminars, or, on certain nights, both. Also, I think most of these so-called motivational books are just scams that made the authors rich, but not the readers. So, instead of books to cheer you up, here's a better, cheaper idea: search for the ruins of Chinese restaurants. When you find one, head for that drawer just under the cash register, the one where they keep all the fortune cookies, and fill up a sack with them, and then, one day, when you come around a giant rock on a beach and see the top of the CN Tower sticking out of the sand, instead of getting all blue and depressed, whip out one of your fortune cookies, crack it open and read, "Soon to meet tall dark strangler. Romance says welcome for coming." That should put a spring in your step.

Now, as for food, I wouldn't bother trying to pack things from home. On your travels across the scarred surface of the planet you'll come across many piles of bricks with giant Loblaws signs sticking out the top. Squeeze your way in and grab some grub. Don't waste your time checking the Best Before dates. Pretty soon, you'll be thrilled to have a can of pork and beans that says "2012/12/21," mostly because it hasn't been opened! So, anyway, that takes care of food. And there you are, ready to face life after the biggest earthquake in the history of the planet, and you and your cat are alive. Hurrah! Now, let's see what you'll be facing if December 21st 2012 brings the biggest flood in a million years.

#2. A Mighty Flood

According to the Bible, this one has been tried before. As the Old Testament reports, God was looking down on His creation one day and noticed that there was way too much wickedness going on, so, being a loving god, he decided to kill everybody on earth by drowning them all, except for a man named Noah and his family. The rest of humanity died in a mighty flood. This way God was able to wipe the slate clean and repopulate the earth, but this time without any wicked people. So, God, how's that workin' for ya so far?

But I digress. What would have to happen for all the lands of the earth to be flooded? Full disclosure here: my knowledge of science is based solely on my years in high school, where the most important thing I learned was from a former Northern Irish rugby player named Mr. Grey who demonstrated how to make things explode by running outside the classroom with a chunk of potassium and dropping it in a bucket of water. Kaboom! On second thought, maybe he did more in Northern Ireland than just play rugby. Anyway, the point is that I'm about to discuss how the entire landmass on earth could be flooded using the scientific know-how of someone who scored a C+ average in high school chemistry.

So in order to get a flood big enough to cover all the continents you would need both the poles and all the glaciers to completely melt, really, really quickly. The best way to speed up the melting would be to double the amount of feed we give to cows every day. This would produce double the volume of cow farts that, as we all know by now, are destroying the ozone layer. That's a scientific fact. The second event to help get enough water to completely flood the planet is for something to happen that would break open all the underground aquifers, which means we'd be flooding the continents with a mix of Evian, Perrier, and San Pellegrino, producing what could be a delightfully refreshing way to drown. Third, all the rain hanging in clouds above us would all have to come down in a once-in-a-lifetime downpour, finally providing a resounding "yes" to those jerks who keep asking "Wet enough for ya?" Finally, the creeks will rise. I realize that, if there is a God, letting the creeks rise is not something God would be willing to do, but they will anyway. And there you have it. All the land on earth would be flooded. This is one of the possible outcomes of the Mayan Calendar coming to a stop on December 21st, 2012.

So, what to do? How do you assure yourself that you can survive this massive washout? Well, for starters, this would be the perfect time to take those swimming lessons you've been promising yourself you'd take for years. I realize it might be somewhat embarrassing to be the only forty-year-old in a class of toddlers learning to dog paddle, but it might just save your life when you're up to your armpits in the mighty torrent. At the very least, if you still don't know how to swim, buy a Tilley hat even if you are not a white-bearded man over sixty. The

Tilley hat is designed to float. It may just keep you afloat long enough for the Coast Guard to pick you up, plus the Tilley hat offers you a waterproof pocket where you can keep a twenty dollar bill, meaning that after the flood waters have receded and the all-clear has sounded, you'll be one of the few survivors with enough money to buy a celebratory Big Mac with fries and a soft drink. You should also equip your home with life vests, and once you have determined that a planet-destroying flood is underway, stand up in front of your family, pull on a life vest and repeat the following announcement while, at the same time, demonstrating how the vest works:

"In case of the unlikely event of the earth being flooded, we would like your attention for the following safety announcement. Life vests are located beneath the couch and La-Z-Boy recliners of the living room as well as under each of the dining room chairs. Remove the vest from the pouch by pulling on the tab. Place the vest over your head, and fasten the straps to the front of the vest. Adjust the straps loosely around your waist. As you leave the house, inflate the vest by pulling down on the red tabs, or manually inflate by blowing into the tubes on either side. Do not inflate your life vest inside the house. This house is equipped with three emergency exits (*use your arms in a broad sweeping motion here*) one at the front, one at the rear, and two over the garage. Operation and use of the exits are illustrated in the safety information card stuck to the front of the fridge. Please take the time to read it and locate the nearest exit to you. Thank you for your attention. Now sit back and enjoy the greatest flood of all time."

You will need to get a boat of some sort. A kayak is pretty useless because you'd only have room for a sandwich and a banana. A canoe would be better, but they're not great for standing up in when you are waving frantically at passing ships. If you own a proper boat, well, good for you, but you'll have to live close enough to the yacht club to get out of there in an emergency. I recommend a Transport Canada-approved four-person life raft. They're easy to store in your front hall closet but, please note, do not inflate them until you get out of the house.

Here's something really important to do to save yourself from the flood: stay up late one night, after midnight, and watch for the TV infomercial that sells Popeil's Pocket Fisherman. This is a TV product that has thrilled generations of insomniacs, and I believe it's still only $19.95. I also believe that operators are still standing by. Here's where this handy little device, with a handle that doubles as a mini tackle box, could save your life in a major flood: you may have grabbed a few bags of trail mix and some granola bars as you ran out the door to inflate your life raft, but, believe me, you will need serious nourishment as the days and maybe weeks go by at sea. You will need to catch fish to eat and there's nothing better than Popeil's Pocket Fisherman to do the job. First, it literally fits in your pocket, leaving your hands free to get life vests on, launch your boat, or even engage pirates in hand-to-hand fighting. Second, you can't find anything better to eat than fish. It's chock full of protein, vitamins, minerals, and omega-3 fatty acids. And you have the biggest ocean in history to drop your line into.

Last but not least, keep your spirits up. Invite your family members to answer you with, "Aye, Cap'n!" and address them with "Avast me hearties!" or "Shiver me timbers!" It'll keep everyone in stitches even when all hope seems lost.

#3. A Mighty Cataclysmic Pole Shift

This theory is very solid. I first heard about it during a lecture at Simon Fraser University, or, maybe it was from a guy sitting on the sidewalk outside the Robson Street liquor store. Hmm. Yeah, it had to have been at SFU. Anyway, what happens during a cataclysmic pole shift is that the combined gravitational effects of the moon and the sun make the earth's crust shift, and the two poles move toward the equator. Geez, you know, maybe it was the guy outside the Robson Street liquor store.

The pole shift theory is easy to believe because we have evidence that, at one time, the Canadian north was home to steaming hot jungles. In fact, in 1999, they found dinosaur tracks in the Yukon and, of course, everyone in Alberta knows about their history with dinosaurs, I mean besides the Conservative Party. I'm talking here about cold-blooded, slimy creatures that ruthlessly stomped on smaller creatures. Okay, I see the confusion with the Conservative Party. So, if this is what happens on December 21st, what are we to do? There is a very easy solution to this: right away you should book Air North Flight 506 from Vancouver to Inuvik, then hop on

Aklak Air Flight 403 to Tuktoyaktuk, that delightful little Inuit hamlet on the Arctic Ocean. Once you arrive, find yourself a real estate agent, I believe his name is Pukkeenegak, and tell him you want to buy all the beach-front property in Tuktoyaktuk. Yes, he will have a good old-fashioned Inuit giggle about it but, eventually, he'll draw up the papers and, just like that, you will be the lucky land baron of "The New Miami Beach,"— well, starting December 22nd, 2012 that is. Then you start running ads in *Zoomer* magazine that say, "Retire to the tropics. Buy a beachfront condo for only $150,000." In no time at all, you'll have every baby boomer still moving without a walker, waddling up in their white buck shoes and black knee socks and slamming down their cold, hard plastic, snapping up your delightful seaside homes with "great views of the Pingos." If you'd like to make even more money, open a chain of parka and mukluk stores in San Diego and just watch the money pour in—well, once those poles shift.

#4. A Mighty Hard-Braking Stop to the Spinning Earth

Why this would happen I'm not sure, but the Mayans were clever devils so who knows what they've got up their sleeve once that calendar of theirs runs out. If the earth stops spinning, the most immediate danger, of course, is that gravity will stop working and people will begin floating upwards, going "where no man has gone before," although no one pictured earthlings exploring the universe in sweat pants and tank tops.

If you really want to survive this disaster, you'll need a good, sturdy tether anchored deep in your back garden. In fact, if you're quick about it and start a company that makes tethers, you'll be the queen of a post-apocalyptic world. When I talk about tethers, I'm not referring to the curly phone-cord tethers that people attach to toddlers in shopping malls. I'm talking about industrial tethers like one-inch Nylon 12-rope with a tensile strength of 110,000 pounds, enough to stop even most obese humans from floating off into space. If you are in the three-hundred-to-four-hundred-pound range, this might be the best incentive you've ever had to lose weight, not getting sucked up skyward like a Delta IV Heavy rocket. One consideration, though: at a certain point, let's say you were a six-hundred-pound human being, you might actually be heavy enough to not float upwards, which sadly, might give people the greatest incentive in modern history to try and consume thirty-thousand calories a day in muffins, burgers, back ribs and twenty-ounce sodas. Still, most people would float away so get yourself, right now, into the tether business, and on December 21st they'll flock, or float, to your stores.

There is also another lucrative enterprise that could make you rich as a result of the earth's sudden stop: selling concrete boots. These are boots weighing over three-hundred pounds each and they will certainly keep you grounded, although they will make running for a bus nearly impossible. The Mafia has perfected this type of footwear for decades in an effort to grant many people their last wish of swimming with the fishes. They sold an excellent pair to Jimmy Hoffa as I recall. Being a sharing and caring organization, the Mafia would probably cut you a nice piece of the action from their cement shoes business. Overall, the fact is that, besides swarms of pedestrians drifting lazily up into the stratosphere along with trash cans, dogs, patio furniture, and plastic children's toys, when the earth stops spinning, life will actually still be pretty normal. So, as long as you can find a way to stay attached to terra firma, you'll be okay. It might even be a bonus health benefit to those of you with arthritic knees.

#5. A Mighty Atomic Blast

As far as I can see, this would have to come from somewhere on earth. Maybe the Iranians will finally perfect a nuclear missile attack, or, as George W. Bush called them, " nu-cu-lar attacks." Unfortunately, due to failed missile tests in recent years, the Iranians will have to drop the warhead off the back of an ox cart because all their missile tests have hit so far are some public toilets, a falafel stand, and a loudspeaker truck playing propaganda songs.

So, if it is a nuclear bomb on December 21st, 2012, how do you survive that? We can thank the Cold War in the 1960s for giving us the answer. During the 1960s, school children in

Canada had to participate in nuclear attack drills. They were trained to "duck and cover" whenever they heard air raid sirens going off. They were instructed to duck under their school desks because, thanks to painstaking research, scientists discovered that the only substance that would protect humans from a nuclear blast was the top part of a wooden school desk.

Although it remains somewhat of a mystery, scientists believe the top of the school desk gained its protective powers because of a combination of the wood (Eastern White Pine), the intricate patterns of the graffiti carved into the top, and the varieties of gum stuck to the underside. As a result, a wooden school desk can protect the person under it from atomic bomb blasts of up to five hundred megatons or more. A megaton, by the way, is a scientific word meaning "huge ton." Because of their almost magical protective powers against atomic explosions, old wooden school desks are now used extensively by our modern military.

For example, did you know that all of NATO's tanks are made entirely from recycled wooden school desks, the inkwell hole being where the tank driver sits with only his head sticking out? Next time you're watching war footage on TV, wait for a close-up of a tank and try and spot the grain of the wood, the intriguing graffiti, and all the tiny chunks of chewing gum stuck to it. For the survival of you and your family against a nuclear bomb, I would advise you to immediately head to a demolition sale at an old school, or go to an auction, and get an old wooden school desk for each member of your family and never again have to worry about surviving a nuclear blast.

#6. A Mighty Freezing of the Earth

This is often referred to as "The Canadian Apocalypse" because Canada has winter twelve months of the year. This is one of the easier life-ending scenarios to survive for Canadians, because they've had so much practice. Canadian children, early on, learn how to build snow forts, and that kind of experience will be invaluable in preparing your accommodation for the coming eternal winter. Also, we've got the clothes, footwear, toques, earmuffs and a full range of attractive long underwear at our disposal in stores around every corner and up your block. We've even got specialists from the Prairie provinces who, because they are the only ones who know how to drive in snow, can get us around safely while the whole earth is frozen over.

The frozen earth ending doesn't actually have to be the end of human life because, if you load up your larder with lots of hearty soups and chili, you can last a long time. The hardest part of the frozen earth scenario is that you will not be able to head south for the winter, as the south will also be frozen over. To help overcome the feelings of depression that will come from not being able to fly to the tropics or the desert, keep a box full of photos from various trips to Maui, or Miami, or

Palm Springs. Also, take a lesson from the Inuit: one of the best things you can do to survive this frozen apocalypse is to buy some dogs, preferably mid-sized with thick fur. Huskies would work well here, so would Malamutes, or even Norwegian Elkhounds. Long ago, the Inuit of Canada's Arctic learned that to survive at various temperatures plus the wind, or as they call it in Toronto, "the windshield factor," a certain number of dogs added to the family grouping could provide enough heat to get you through the night. On a cold night, one dog would be fine. On an extra cold night, two dogs would be needed, and when Mother Nature throws all the winds and freezing temperatures at you, three dogs would be needed inside the igloo, thus the term "a three dog night." With the whole planet in a deep freeze, every night would be a three-dog night. The bonus is, you and the family and the three dogs will have a jolly time belting out "Jeremiah was a Bullfrog!" all night long.

Let's briefly deal with other possible calamities that could befall us on December 21st, based on the biblical Seven Plagues of Egypt. All the Bible fans will remember that back about three thousand years ago, God had a pretty short temper and was constantly coming up with ways to kill off naughty people. I'm rather skeptical it will be one of these plagues because they're pretty old-fashioned ideas. However I do want to be thorough, and on the ever-so-slightest chance that one of these happens again on December 21st, let's quickly look at some of the "plagues" and talk about how you can survive them.

#7. A Mighty Plague of Frogs

This might include "all manner of amphibians," which means that you could get a downpour of frogs, toads, salamanders, and even the odd newt. The best way to survive a plague of frogs is to sign up for French cooking classes and learn how to prepare frog's legs, especially sautéed and accompanied by a chilled bottle of Chablis. While others are drowning in heaps of dead frogs, you'll be chowing down for years to come.

#8. A Mighty Swarm of Flies

Buy screens for all your windows and stay indoors. Stock up on fly swatters and get that sticky fly paper you can hang from the ceiling. With these weapons, you'll easily survive an attack from a swarm of flies.

#9. A Mighty Hailstorm

It depends on what type of hailstorm could hit the planet. If the hailstones are the size of golf balls, stay indoors. If your car is parked on the street, prepare for a call to your local body shop. If the hailstones are the size of grapefruit, you should head for the storm cellar, or at least your basement rec room, until it subsides. Have a list of local roofers handy for when the hail stops. If the hailstones are the size of beach balls, stay in the rec room and have a good read of your home insurance policy, because you will be needing a new one.

#10. A Mighty Swarm of Gnats

See #8. Plus stock up on Deep Woods Off because gnats include midges, no-see-ums, sandflies, and blackflies. They can bite, so coat your entire body with Off. Without getting too kinky, help your neighbours slather the repellant over their entire bodies too.

#11. A Mighty Plague of Boils

This might seem a minor calamity to happen at the end of the Mayan Calendar, compared to things like earthquakes and floods, but boils can be very nasty little puss-filled bumps, similar to a plague of Rush Limbaughs. The best way to survive a plague of boils on the earth is for each human to obey one simple rule: never lance a boil yourself. Only doctors can do this, but because there'll be billions of people lined up at walk-in clinics around the world, it'll be hard to find a doctor. So just cover the boils with clean bandages and wait for the puss to drain by itself.

#12. A Mighty Plague of Locusts

Don't let the name fool you. These are just grasshoppers, and rather than run from them in fear, get out your snow shovel and start scooping them up. They will make an excellent, protein-filled meal to help you pass time during the apocalypse, or, as I like to say, a nice light snack. Frying grasshoppers is the best way to cook them, but first, make sure you pull the head off and remove the guts and stomach. You'll all agree: they do taste like chicken and they make a nice accompaniment to your frog's legs.

#13. A Mighty Spurting of Blood From Your Eyes

I've also included this as a possible way the world could end, even though the chances of it happening are very, very slim. However, because it's featured on the front cover of this book, I thought it best not to confuse people by leaving it out. Blood spurting out the eyes is a rare eye disorder, although, admittedly, a very alarming one. The name for this medical condition is "plasmasquirtopticitis."

Ophthalmologists cannot say what causes the relentless streaming of blood through the eye sockets, which can spray innocent bystanders as far away as twelve feet. The only way to stop it is by use of a tourniquet pulled tightly around the circumference of the head just below the nose and held there until the blood begins to coagulate in the eye sockets, usually after about two hours, at which point surgeons will usually pack the eye sockets with wadding and leave it for about two weeks or until the crisis has passed. This is a difficult enough procedure with just one patient, never mind three billion of them. Doctors would be instantly overwhelmed by the surgery required, never mind the fact that it would be a huge drain on the world supply of wadding. The idea that every human on earth could, all at the same time, begin gushing blood from the eyes seems unlikely, but, as I say, no one knows what the Mayans had in mind with the end of the calendar, so it's best to be prepared even for this very odd ending to life.

Points to Ponder from the chapter "Possible World Endings And How To Survive Them"

When I was a choirboy, I would constantly repeat the words "World without end. Amen." But I never really thought about what the words meant, probably because, as I was saying them, I was staring down at Amanda Bickell in the first pew, waiting for her to uncross her legs. As a result, the implications of "world without end" never really stuck in my head. So, here I am all those years later and it's finally starting to hit home; the world's going to end and Amanda Bickell never did uncross her legs. I lost on both counts. Don't you wish you had paid more attention to things when you were young?

4.

It's Gone? The Hell You Say!

First, the bad news: despite the myriad of helpful tips I've given out in this book to ward off the various upheavals, downpours, floodings, freezings, and death rays, most life on Planet Earth will die when the Mayan Calendar ends, and, odds are, that includes you. So it's best to, as doctors are so fond of saying when death is near, "prepare the family." For example, after reading my tips you may have bet on the earth being hit by a downpour of frogs and installed frog-proof siding on your house. But, instead, when the Mayan Calendar ends, the earth's molten core may come shooting out of all the manholes, against which your frog-proof siding will have little or no effect; ergo, you'll be a goner.

First and most important, let me assure you, and I'm backed up by the highest authorities at the Vatican when I tell you this: if you are concerned because you think you might break

As the family gathered for their last meal before disaster struck the earth, the boys were smirking but Nana couldn't see anything funny about the end of the Mayan Calendar.

one or more of the Ten Commandments just before the cataclysm strikes, there is good news. No matter what bad things you have done in your life, from having sex with the maid in the California governor's mansion, to trying to sell Barack Obama's senate seat, or spending money from the G8 budget to build a gazebo in your hometown, there is very comforting news for you: there is no Hell. It's gone. It used to exist, yes, from the beginning of time. For thousands of generations, it was part of the yin and yang of living—heaven and hell, the good and the bad, white hats and black, Liberals and Conservatives.

When people died in the old days, if they had been "iffy-bad," they went to Purgatory first, which was very much like sitting in a doctor's waiting room reading magazines so old you have to lean over to the person next to you and say, "You have any idea what this Watergate thing is that they're talking about?" Well, Purgatory used to be like that, and the point of it was that some people had done bad things but not bad enough to be sent directly to Hell, so they were made to wait in Purgatory while somebody in power went through the evidence before pronouncing them Hell-bound or otherwise. This whole system worked really well, especially as a deterrent to young children who were told by their loving parents that if they didn't finish their dinner, the Devil would take them into his fiery cave where Uncle Art went after being charged with shoplifting at Woolworth's.

Hell and Purgatory kept everybody walking the straight and narrow, until 1999, that is, and that fateful July day when Pope John Paul the Second, the spokesperson for God on earth, officially announced to the whole world that there was no Hell. He had caught everybody in the afterlife completely off guard. No memos, no warnings, not even a quick phone call to somebody up there to say, "Okay guys, I've decided to get rid of Hell." Officials in the netherworld went ballistic, according to an official of the afterlife, speaking on condition of anonymity. It's completely understandable that they would have blown their tops over this, because, while it was easy for the Pope to just say, "Okay, people, there's no Hell anymore," it was everybody in the sweet hereafter who had to carry out the orders. There were a lot of angry souls over there who had to start the massive job of dismantling Hell. No easy task. First they had to get rid of millions of instruments of torture, and Hell had the best of anyone. They had miles of dungeons loaded with devices like the pendulum, the rack, the breast ripper, the spanish tickler, crocodile shears, foot roasters, knee splitters, even waterboarding rooms. Hell was like going to the biggest and best gym in town. They had every machine a cruel torturer would ever want, way better than anything Vlad the Impaler or Dick Cheney ever had.

All these torture devices had to be melted down, because you couldn't sell this stuff. You couldn't put an ad on Craigslist saying "One used Chair of Torture for sale, in good working condition. Includes instruction booklet personally signed by Idi Amin." And, let's face it, these things don't look good in any room of your house. I've never seen Debby Travis surprise some unsuspecting couple with a makeover that features a family room with a head crusher sitting in the corner next to the fireplace.

So, because all these torture tools wouldn't be of interest to anyone, except a few Somali warlords or Canada Revenue Agency auditors, they had to melt down all the torture tools and sell them to scrap metal dealers. Then, they had the unenviable job of extinguishing the eternal flames. If you think it's tough getting out of a contract for your house with your local natural gas supplier, try telling them they're about to lose a contract worth ninety million shekels a month, the shekel being the historic currency of the Great Beyond. So figure it out in your own currency and see how upset the gas company would be. For example, one shekel equals 0.277970683 Canadian dollars. So multiply that by ninety million, and that is one scary phone call to the natural gas dealer. I don't know who got to make that call, but we know it wasn't the Pope.

Another huge job in demolishing Hell was finding a new place for all the lawyers to go to, as lawyers made up most of the population in Hell at that time, followed by financial advisors, car salesmen, and telemarketers. Eventually it was decided that all the lawyers who had been in Hell would go back to earth but could only work *pro bono*, which, truth be told, was worse than Hell for a lawyer. Then all the land had to be sold, the fifty-six billion hectares known as The Hades Projects, or just "The Projects." Unlike the instruments of torture, they had no problem selling the land. It was snapped up immediately by a syndicate of Beijing millionaires who started building luxury, high-end condos with the tag line, "It's a Hell of a place to live!" The prices ranged from six hundred thousand for a one-bedroom with a garden view, up to $6.5 million for a penthouse with 360 degree views of Uranus, Neptune and Jupiter. Because the condos were marketed to Chinese buyers, every building had the same address, #888, so for most people it was still Hell to find your way around.

As to the CEO of Hell, once the Pope had declared Hell no longer existed, the Devil had to be laid off. He was escorted, unceremoniously, to the Gates of Hell and told that the stuff in his office would be sent to him later. He wasn't out of work long, though. At the end of 1999, he was headhunted by Goldman Sachs and we all know how well things turned out there. The Devil still works for them by the way. You'll find him in the details.

And so, you can rest easier if you are blown to smithereens when the Mayan Calendar ends, because there is nothing but Heaven waiting for you on the other side, although, with Hell gone, you'll be a little upset to bump into Adolph Hitler, Pol Pot, and Osama bin Laden sitting around on a cloud, eating Philadelphia Cream Cheese, discussing their feelings. However, there will be many surprises in store for you once Charon the ferryman has delivered you to the other side of the River Styx. That's what the next chapter is all about.

Points to Ponder about the chapter "It's Gone? The Hell You Say!"

The truth is that even though the Pope said Hell doesn't exist anymore, he was referring to the after-death variety Hell. In fact, there's plenty of hells right here on earth. Try calling your cable company when your cable signal disappears. They will have you on hold for an hour while they play "A Horse With No Name" over and over until the up-talking geek finally comes on line. That is Hell! Or how about you go through airport security having taken off your shoes, belt, etc, and the alarm goes off, making the surly security woman zap you up and down and sideways until she zeroes in on the wire in your brassiere which she keeps wanding over and over. How's that for Hell? Or even going through the drugstore checkout when one of your items won't scan, at which point the clerk picks up the store intercom and says, "Could I have a price check on Depends, Super Pack of fifty?" Give me an Amen on Hell on earth.

After a close vote, the Barking-on-Mersey Men's Lawn Bowling Team voted to display their secret weapons for overcoming the end of the world, the powerful and shiny Shields of Destiny.

5.
Heaven, I'm In Heaven

So if you bite the big one when the Mayan Calendar ends, there's now great relief in knowing that the Vatican cancelled Hell over twelve years ago. And there's even more good news if you kick the bucket on December 21st, 2012: there really is a heaven, or, more precisely, heavens. Here, finally, is the proof mankind has been waiting for since the arrival of the greatest thing ever, opposing thumbs, which was followed closely by sliced bread, made all the more appealing because you now had opposing thumbs to get it buttered. Based on what you've been told, most of you imagine that life after death is pretty straightforward. You know, you are met at the end of a long dark tunnel by Jesus or Mohammed, surrounded by a posse of your ancestors and departed family members, and they lead you into this gleaming city where there is no such thing as garbage trucks, parking meters that don't work, shivering people hanging around the front doors of office buildings smoking cigarettes, or bike couriers who break all traffic laws while giving you the finger. A city without any of that sounds like a lovely place, but it's not exactly true, although I like the "no bike couriers" part.

Heaven is not as simple as you have been led to believe by your religions. What they tell you is just spin, much like when a major corporation makes a huge blunder and, instead of sending out the CEO to face the media, they send out a well-coiffed, glib spokesperson who got her Bachelor of Bafflegab from the U of T. To get you the actual truth about what happens after you have started pushing up daisies, you have to communicate with those who have gone to the other side before us, the spirits of people who have already crossed the River Styx, gone through death's door, have two feet in the grave, or have simply popped their clogs.

This "proof" of life after death comes entirely from one of the best authorities on the subject of talking with the departed. Edgar Cayce was really good, but these days no one can touch the psychic abilities of the world-famous oracle Auntie Phlegm. Despite her worldwide fame, she still operates a humble little shop at 34th and Vine in Manhattan's Tarot Card District. You can easily tell her shop apart from all the other fortunetellers' shops because Auntie Phlegm's establishment has a large neon hand glowing in the front window. Auntie Phlegm has operated her psychic business there for over thirty years and has become a recognized celebrity on the streets of the Big Apple, giving private readings to the likes of Pope Benedict, Margaret

Thatcher, Boris Yeltsin, Pee Wee Herman, Mother Teresa, Sid Vicious, The Dalai Lama, Boy George, Osama bin Laden, and Dickie Duff, just to mention a few of the world figures who dropped by for a séance with dead loved ones.

Old timers who visited Manhattan in the 1960s might be confused, because there was another similar type of establishment at 34th and Vine that was run by Madame Ruth, you know, that gypsy with a gold-capped tooth. Police shut down her shop in the late 60s and charged her with selling little bottles of black market liquid Viagra. Auntie Phlegm moved in shortly after and has been there ever since. I had a choice of two ways to get this information about the different paradises from Auntie Phlegm: one was to grease her palm with silver, but there are no coins in circulation these days with silver in them, and fortune tellers do not like it when you grease their palms with nickel-plated steel. So I chose the other method—greasing her palm with my VISA, and purchasing the rights to quote from her landmark book on séances entitled *I Enjoy My Spirits*.

Unlike other psychics, who merely commune with the dead, some years ago Auntie Phlegm decided to carry out a scientific study. With each disembodied soul she communed with, she specifically asked what their religion was while they were in the physical world and had them describe what the surroundings in their afterlife looked like. The result was her groundbreaking book which clearly shows us that, depending on your beliefs, there are a number of different places you can end up in after you die. In order to save space, I've included only the four major religions in the world that make up seventy per cent of the earth's population. The other smaller religions, like Sikhism, Judaism, the Bahá'í Faith, Animism, Shintoism, the Rastafari movement, and even the silliest of them all, Scientology, a tiny religion only for Hollywood actors based entirely on a sci-fi novel and written by the son of the well-known nursery rhyme character, Old Mother Hubbard.

Auntie Phlegm has offered all of you a one-time offer to come in for a séance and get a preview of where you'll be heading if you happen to buy the farm when the Mayan Calendar ends in 2012. Hurry in now and receive fifty per cent off the séance, plus a coupon for any appetizer at Georgio's House of Spanakopita, located just next door to Auntie Phlegm's. Or you could just buy yourself a copy of Auntie Phlegm's bestseller, *I Enjoy My Spirits*, published by Bendover and Kopff, available wherever books are sold.

#1. Heaven for True Christians

We start with this type of heaven because Christians do make up the largest religion in the world with 2.1 billion members, then Muslims with 1.57 billion, all the way down to the smallest religion in the world, "The Church of LeBron James" who is a forward with the NBA's Miami Heat. Not only is he the only member of the church, but he also believes he is God Almighty. But I digress. Auntie Phlegm notes, in her book, that of all the séances she conducted, she never actually talked to a true Christian. So, if you believe you are a true Christian, i.e. you love every person on earth, even your enemies, you forgive everyone for anything that's ever been done to you, you have never said a bad word about anyone, or had a bad thought about anyone and you've never lied, stolen or cheated, then when the Mayan Calendar ends and you die, you will *not* be met on the other side by Jesus. You ARE Jesus!

#2. Heaven for Not-So-True Christians

This includes all Christians with the exception of the above mentioned. Auntie Phlegm reports that the good news for all of you is that your heaven is filled with beautiful churches with shiny spires. The streets are paved with gold and all the lamp poles have speakers mounted on them playing hymns sung by the Mormon Tabernacle Choir, all day long. The bad news is you are required to spend twelve hours a day sitting on hard wooden pews and, half of that time, on kneelers that have really skimpy padding. Even though there is supposed to be no pain in your heaven, you'll find yourself grunting as you get up from the marathon daily church services and wishing the Swedish Touch practitioners hadn't gone to that other heaven where all the exotic dancers go. Still, if you can handle "Onward Christian Soldiers" blasting through the streets 24/7, she reports it's not a bad place to be.

#3. Heaven for Muslims

The Koran says that Muslim "paradise" features rivers of wine and harems of virgins, where every martyred man gets seventy-two virgins plus seventy-two wives and happiness forever. Auntie Phlegm says that is not true, based on the spirits of dead Muslims she talked to, and how could it be? Show me any man who has to manage, for all eternity, a house filled with a hundred and forty-four women and I will show you a man who is exhausted, worn out, fed up, and dealing with a throbbing headache. It's enough to make him wish for a night out with the boys, or at least, to head down to one of those rivers of wine and take a long drink.

No, Auntie Phlegm's Muslim deceased all say that the actual Islamic paradise makes the most sense of any of the heavens up there. In order to balance out the injustices of earthly life, in Muslim paradise, the sexes are reversed. If you were a Muslim man on earth, after you die, you become a Muslim woman and are forced to wear an unflattering, sweaty-smelling tent all day long and cover your face. You are also not allowed to drive a car, get a job, go to the gym, and certainly not hang out with the boys at the local espresso café. According to Auntie Phlegm, women in Muslim paradise are the happiest creatures in the universe because they can do anything they want without their spouse's permission. Auntie Phlegm also says that something very similar happens to Mormons.

#4. Heaven for Hindus, Buddhists, and Taoists

Because members of these religions believe in instant reincarnation after death, i.e. spending one life as a human, dying, then returning as a goldfish, the powers that be decided to keep costs down by creating something resembling a large airport waiting area, filled with many people sleeping on seats and on the floor. She says the washrooms smell and are completely out of toilet paper, the flight screen continues to flash "Delayed – Retardé," the TV screens all keep playing the same four credit card commercials over and over, the only food available is from a machine that has run out of everything except salted peanuts, and there are a large number of babies and toddlers that are screaming their little heads off. What this means is that when you get that call many hours later that says "Paging Air Hindu passenger Mr. Bagwanti, your flight back to earth is leaving in ten minutes!" you will be more than ready to get out of there.

#5. Heaven for Atheists.

I know, I know…an oxymoron. But, as millions of dead atheists have discovered over the centuries, there is an afterlife after all. Besides, there are 1.1 billion admitted atheists on earth at the moment, so they deserve to be included. What does Auntie Phlegm say will happen to an atheist who kicks the bucket on December 21st, 2012? It sounds great to me. First, of course, you'll be floating in the air, looking down on your body as paramedics try to lift the piano off you that has fallen from fifteen floors during the earthquake. Eventually you will find yourself travelling down a long dark tunnel. This will continue on and on and on, eventually forcing you to think that you are being punished for not believing in God, then, after what seems like an eternity of zipping down this dark tunnel, you are deposited on your butt in a pitch black room where you end up sitting on a cold, bare floor. Everything is silent, not a sound, and just as you are resigning yourself to spending forever in this lonely cell, all the lights go on in a blinding flash, a crowd screams "Surprise!," and there's God and Jesus and Moses and the whole gang, laughing, blowing on noisemakers and popping open champagne bottles. That's when you smile and say, "I'm a believer!"

Points to ponder from the chapter "Heaven, I'm in Heaven"

One thing that I didn't mention in this chapter is that, because it is the Mayan Calendar that will cause the end of the world on December 21st, 2012, it's possible that everyone who dies will go into the Mayan Underworld. If this is the case, be prepared. When the Pope declared the end of Hell, he meant the Christian Hell. The Mayans did not get the memo, and so, unfortunately, they still have a hell. It's called the underworld city of Xibalba, and it's filled with six weird houses, kind of like a Mesoamerican Carnival with scary attractions like "Razor House" with all sorts of blades zipping around and "Bat House" where you have to deal with shrieking bats. I'm not saying this is where you'll go after the Grim Reaper catches you at the end of the Mayan Calendar, but it might be good to learn a few words of Mayan. Here's a phrase I picked up, "Woqan hin k'al ay max ek'k'u" which means, in ancient Mayan, "I spent the entire day sitting down." I'm not sure how that might benefit you in the Mayan underworld, but I wish you luck just the same.

As the Mayan Calendar ended, Peter was oblivious to the fact that his sister had become a zombie and the dog had turned into a pumpkin.

6.

How To Talk To Your Children About The Annihilation Of Earth

First, no matter what age the children are, all parents must stop using that dumb expression, "Now, now. Stop crying. It's not the end of the world." Yes it is, so find another reason for your child to stop crying. How about, "Now, now. Stop crying. Forty-year-olds are not supposed to be living with their parents." The best way to tackle the sensitive topic of explaining to your children that human life is about to come to a horrible end is to divide the explanations into age groupings, because the approach used will differ based on the age and education level of the child. Some children, for example, are only capable of speaking in monosyllables, such as fifteen-year-old boys.

So let's start with explaining to toddlers about the end of the world. To define a toddler, I'm going to use the Hardy-Laurel Toddling Principle that "a toddler is a human who walks with a toddling gait," toddling being a style of walking requiring the legs to be spread apart and simply lifted and slammed down as you go forward, coming to rest when you fall headfirst into a bookshelf. Toddlers, on average, learn only by taste and pain, tasting everything from plastic toys to crusty cat excrement, and then the aforementioned pain of that head-first fall into the bookshelf. So, how to explain to your toddler that the world will be engulfed by flames or drowned or blown apart, whichever one it is, on December 21st, 2012. Well, stand down. You're off the hook if you have a toddler. There is no way a human with a vocabulary of "Da-da," "poo-poo," "pee-pee," and "good girl," can comprehend the concept of tectonic lithosphere plates being massively overlain by either or both of two types of crustal material. "Pee-pee" will be the result for all of us, of course, but really, it's way beyond the grasp of a toddler, so relax. Save yourself for the birds and bees speech, if you're all still alive when that time comes.

Next, how do you explain to a kindergarten-age child about the coming apocalypse? Kindergarten-age children require simple explanations to everything because their comprehension is still not far past the embryo stage. However, I advise you not to lie to them. For example, telling children of this age that they came from their mother's stomach might come back to haunt them in later years. High school science class might be one such time when they come to the disgusting realization that if you start out in your mother's stomach, you must then move through her small intestine, then her large intestine, on into her bowels and out her anus, meaning you actually are the little shit that your mother kept calling you after you stayed out 'til 1 a.m. and came home smelling of cheap tequila and taco chips. So don't lie to your kids about the facts of life, or death, as the case may be with the apocalypse. Here's how to explain the End of Days to a kindergarten-age child: simple and with some drama. Go to your nearest Endangered Species store and buy yourself one of their inflatable planet earths. It's essentially a beach ball that looks like earth. Get a piece of string about a foot long. Tie it to the North Pole then start spinning the inflated planet. As it's spinning, tell your child that it's (and here you can insert how many days away from December 21st you are) only fifteen more sleeps until something big is going to happen. Your child will naturally think you're referring to Christmas, but you will say, "No, what I'm talking about is…" And here you stick a pin in the inflated planet, causing an enormous bang that will make your child scream and start crying. Take the deflated lump of plastic that was the planet earth and hang it like a mobile from the ceiling of your child's bedroom. Leave there until the earth finally does explode, implode, melt, flood, or whatever. Believe me, you will have the only young child nodding knowingly as the cataclysm washes across our planet.

Next, let's deal with how to talk to a ten-year-old about the end of times on our planet. Ten-year-olds are very much into games and it's through these games that you can best communicate the eradication of all human life. Ten-year-old boys, for example, are totally obsessed with games like Final Fantasy on their PS3. Pause the game and tell them to stop whining because Sephiroth needs his help in a battle against Rufus Shinra. This will get his attention. Tell your ten-year-old that a shelter needs to be built under the basement stairs to protect everyone against the coming evil. Your ten-year-old boy will spring into action, taking up hammer and nails, and will be fully occupied right up until the Apocalypse strikes. The bonus is you'll have a half-decent shelter in case it turns out to be massive earthquakes. For ten-year-old girls, it's even easier. At ten they have become fascinated with makeup. They don't put it on too well, of course, often ending up looking like Britney Spears just after closing time at the Boom Boom Room. Men, wait until your wife is napping then get your ten-year-old daughter to take a new tube of lipstick, I would pick Revlon Fire and Ice, and have your daughter begin slathering it onto your sleeping wife's face, lots all over the lips, but also some good patches on the cheeks and even across the brow and down the neck. When your wife finally wakes up and gets the fright of her life looking in the mirror, tell your daughter that's how mommy will look on December 21st, 2012, when the Mayan Calendar ends. Message sent. Over and out!

Finally, let's give you the tools you'll need to tell your

teenager about Armageddon. First, it's silly to try and have a conversation with a teen. Something like, "What would be the worst thing you can imagine happening in your life?" for example, because the answer will always be "Not getting a signal on my cellphone?" If you want to communicate anything to a teenager, there is only one way: send them a text. This will come as no surprise, I'm sure, but teenagers never, ever lift their eyes off the screens of their phones for more than ten seconds, believing that they might miss an incoming text, and this is exactly where you'll have their rapt attention, I guarantee it.

First, you'll need an alias. This kind of thing is done every day on the Internet where nobody is actually who they say they are, which allows them to be outrageously rude, mean, and libelous because no one can sue "anonymous." Besides, if your teen gets a text from "Mom" or "Dad," they're not likely to respond. I suggest using the handle "Dude." Teens are so dimwitted they are always fooled by this and end up thinking you are one of them. They will reply instantly. Okay, so you have become "Dude" and you need to send your teen the first text of your plan to explain how the end of the world is coming on December 21st. Please don't deviate from what I am writing here. Copy everything exactly as I have written it.

Your opening text should say, "Dude sup." They will reply with the standard teen response, "sup." This is the breakthrough you're been waiting for, so get right to your first volley in the plan to alert them about the upcoming destruction of the world. Type this: "dec 21st, 2012." That's pretty obvious. They will reply with "QL" which means, "cool." Okay, they're playing along. Next, type in "mayan calNdA." You can guess what that means. They'll reply with, "K." So far so good. Then the big one. Type, "it's ll ovr." They will reply with "W@," and that's when you lay it all on them in one powerful sentence. Type "w'r gunA di." They will be quite shaken when they read this and will type in "Dude WTF," and you will end the text communication with these ominous words: "CU on d oder cYd." And, just like that, you will have done it. Your teen will now know that the end of the Mayan Calendar signals the end of everyone's life and they will never know it came from their father or mother or aunt or uncle.

The message will spread like lightning to "Dudes" everywhere and in about thirty seconds, every teen with a cell phone in the Western world will know that the Apocalypse is upon us. Follow all the above instructions to the letter, and you will be able to successfully talk to your children about the coming cataclysm. Unfortunately, I have no suggestions as to how you tell the Canada Revenue Agency you will no longer be paying taxes as of December 22nd, 2012. Good luck with that.

Points to ponder from the chapter "How To Talk To Your Children About The Annihilation Of Earth"

There are going to be people, and I know some of them, who will put off telling their children about this until it's actually happening. I see it all the time. I know fathers and mothers who call themselves "Mommy" and "Daddy" in front of their children even when the children have passed the age of sixty. They are depriving the children of ever knowing the real first names of their parents (In this case, Chuck and Moranica). Or parents who refused to tell their daughters the truth about how babies were made, instead telling them that they could get pregnant from sitting on dirty toilet seats. Their daughters all eventually did become pregnant but, for the rest of their lives, had an unnatural fear of using public toilets. I think children should be told that life is coming to an end on December 21st, 2012, what about you?

As she swung open the front door and heard the terrible news about the world coming to an end, Mary thought to herself, "I should put some makeup on."

7.

Bearers Of Bad Tidings

When you open your front door and look out on December 21st, 2012, you'll notice some things are wrong. First, there's no newspaper. Why? Well, if you had checked the fine print of your subscription you would have noticed it says that the newspaper is not delivered on Sundays, statutory holidays, and the end of the world. The paperboy, like everyone else, is heading for higher ground. The second thing you'll notice is that the man next door, who always dances down his front step whistling the Viagra tune every morning, now rests limply against his steps. He was either too depressed about the Apocalypse to engage in a night of wild monkey dancing, or he buys his Viagra on the Internet and got ripped off with a blue-coloured placebo.

Other things you'll notice that morning will be birds dropping, flames will be shooting out of manholes, and no Mormons will be going door to door. Your natural instinct will tell you that this isn't normal, so you'll rush back and turn on your TV, but, what's this, Oprah's still on, calmly talking with a tearful Paris Hilton about feelings. You flip to HGTV and the two gay guys who decorate bedrooms are coming close to another slap fight. You click on the History Channel and they're showing a re-enactment of the Peloponnesian War using homemade robots. You check out *The View*, but if in fact they are talking about the end of the world, they're all yelling about it at the same time and that makes your brain hurt, so you try FOX News. Of course! Why didn't you think of a news channel? Sadly, FOX News is busy with a panel of Tea Bag Party members discussing why coloreds need their own separate water fountains. "Whatever happened to breaking news?" you yell out, and it becomes painfully obvious that television channels will never break away from their regular programming, even for the destruction of the planet. What to do? There's only one choice: radio. You rush into your bedroom and switch on your bedside radio and, finally, the answers to all your questions are there. Choose any station, actually, because they're all carrying the same programming.

Welcome to Canada's Emergency Alert System. I could tell you what the EAS does in emergencies such as this, but it would be better to just lift it right from the EAS website, which, by the way, you can find online at www.easendoftheworldannouncements.gc.ca. I'll let these folks explain it all to you:

"Here on the EAS website, we can safely say that Canadians should rest assured that when the clock strikes 11:11a.m. Universal Time on December 21st, Canada's Emergency Alert System will spring into action. The EAS will immediately take over the signals of all radio stations in Canada to instruct the population on how to stay alive during the world-ending disaster. This section of our website will familiarize Canadians with the Emergency Alert System. This is the broadcasting juggernaut that will hit the ground running when, in one possible dire example, the earth's core heats up to 100,000 degrees Celsius and magma begins shooting out of toilets. The Emergency Alert System for Canada is located in an abandoned mine shaft, a secure and very top-secret bunker miles below the earth's surface in British Columbia, ready to broadcast at the drop of a hat with a crack team of DJs, news readers, and public service announcers, all highly trained specialists in the art of disaster broadcasting. The DJs were once some of Canada's elite Disc Jockeys. You may even have listened to such ratings winners as Buster and Beaver in the Morning from 99.8 The Rat, or Jim, Gord and the Girl from 88.2 The Heap. You might have wondered why you don't hear them on the radio anymore. Unlike most DJs in Canada, they weren't let go during a regular monthly house cleaning. Instead, they were headhunted by the recruiting team at EAS, and now they're part of the team standing on guard for you at the Emergency Alert System. For them, the term 'DJ' now stands for 'Disaster Jockey.'

"Because of the Canada Security Act, we are restricted in how much we can reveal about this team of broadcast specialists, which has been in place since 1957 during the Cold War, when

Canadians lived in fear of a nuclear attack. Many of the original members of the EAS team are still on staff, although they are quite elderly, as you can imagine, after working in the bunker studio for fifty-four years. This is why recruitment is on-going. Obviously, these superbly trained broadcasters have never been required to step up to the microphone and say, and this is just one of many possible scenarios, "This is the Emergency Alert System, All Calamity All the Time, at eleven hundred hours, eleven minutes, Universal Time on Friday, December 21st. We have received word that, apparently, due to the wickedness of mankind, non-believers in Canada are currently being swallowed by a lake of fire. Stand by for instructions on how to minimize the damage and save lives, but first this commercial message from the makers of Mr. Grease Fire, the only home extinguisher tough enough to put out the biggest stovetop fire you can throw at it.

"The EAS staff has scripts on hand for forty-seven possible endings to life on earth. The above was just an example, as the Canadian government does not endorse any one particular world-ending catastrophe over another, although the large numbers of evangelicals in our government firmly believe that whatever tragedy happens to the earth, it will be God's wrath punishing Liberals for passing legislation allowing gays to marry. Nevertheless, your EAS is prepared for other possible reasons for the earth's destruction."

(Note) Only once did the EAS team come very close to taking over the Canadian airways. In the early hours of January 4th, 1999, over 118 centimetres of snow (that's over forty-six

inches!) had fallen on Toronto, Canada's largest city. Traffic was snarled and schools were closed. It was so serious that the mayor at the time, Mel Lastman, asked the Canadian Army to send troops to shovel the snow because it was beyond the capabilities of Toronto's city workers. What Canadians never knew was that Canada's Defense Minister actually had his hand on the red phone that connects directly to the EAS bunker in B.C. He came within seconds of activating the Emergency Alert System, so serious was that snowfall in Toronto. Obviously the call was never made, and all EAS DJs were ordered to stand down, and went back to rehearsing their emergency bulletins.

In many ways, this group of first-broadcast-responders is similar to fire fighters who sit around with nothing to do for hours on end and then suddenly have to leap into action. In the case of the EAS staff, they have never had to do the important work they have been trained for in fifty-four years, due to a lack of major catastrophes threatening human kind. Every single person working in this secret broadcasting station in the bowels of the earth has been recruited from radio and TV stations across Canada, most receiving a phone call late at night to "see a man about a dog," which is the secret code used by the EAS recruiters to let the DJs or news readers know that they have been called to serve their country. Very few have ever refused the job, mostly due to the lure of massive public service salaries, starting at $500,000 a year plus full benefits and a public service pension payout of over $100,000 per year for the rest of their life (comparable to that of senators, MPs, and PMO staff), regardless of whether the world ends or not. No wonder every disc jockey in Canada hanging around the radio station coffee machine secretly whispers about "seeing a man about a dog.

"Unfortunately, many are called but few are chosen for a career at the Emergency Alert Network. The training is rigorous and the standards are high. DJs, for example, must be able to instantly instruct listeners in how to protect themselves against thundering underground explosions that have created seismic waves which are destroying most of the major Canadian cities, and do it while "hitting the fade" over the opening sixteen instrumental seconds of Michael Buble's "I Haven't Met you Yet." This is well beyond the reach of most disc jockeys! These same DJs receive extensive EAS training on reading announcements about possible flooding, delivered in an alarmed voice, a method used for decades by supper-hour newscasters. Lest we lead you to believe the lifestyle of an EAS broadcaster is glamourous, we should emphasize that their lives are, in fact, very difficult. For example, they must constantly maintain two separate identities: one as emergency DJs on the front lines of disaster broadcasting, the other as mild-mannered, seemingly ordinary citizens of a small town nestled in the western slopes of the Rocky Mountains bordering British Columbia. The name of the town cannot be revealed due to security reasons, as well as a potentially dangerous spike in real estate prices for that little town if Canadians discovered its location and flocked there to try and save themselves from the death of the planet.

"It is here in this town, a town that resembles thousands of other quiet hamlets across Canada, that the secret entrance exists to the elevator shaft that takes these EAS heroes down to work every day. Although, as we say, the name of the town must be kept secret, we can tell you that the entrance to the elevator shaft is in the disabled washroom of a Tim Horton's restaurant, an iconic Canadian restaurant that has at least one location in every Canadian town. The entrance to the abandoned mine shaft requires a special key, unavailable to regular customers, that can only be accessed by asking a Tim Horton's team member for a "Double-double with no cream." Because a Double-double is a coffee with two creams and two sugars, the Tim Horton's team member instantly recognizes the secret codename, and that allows them to turn over the key to the elevator shaft. The double life these broadcasters must live is designed to keep the other citizens in town from becoming suspicious. To ordinary citizens of the town they might appear to be, for example, Frank Smithers, a mild-mannered hockey-card collector from the edge of town, but once he is in place behind the EAS microphone, he is "Disaster Dan, the All-Night Man." Or she might be Gerda Grimsby, a slightly plump, odd-smelling woman from the other side of the river, but once down that shaft, she becomes 'Eagle Eye Evie with your evacuation route traffic conditions!'

"Here at the EAS, we can assure you that once Canadian government officials get wind of the end of the world, they will order regular radio stations and cellular phone carriers to carry the EAS network. This is how it will appear on your cellphone, if you are on, for example, the Virgin cell phone network—they will immediately send you a text saying, 'Hey there! Just a reminder that the End of Days is under way. How cool is that? Love! The Virgin Team.' The EAS will also send out Twitter messages warning all citizens that the earth is about to be destroyed...in 140 characters or less. It might be good right now to start following the Emergency Alert System on Twitter, even though their tweets are very low-key at the moment and not too frequent, for example, 'Human life still safe. For now. But we'll be here for you when it all goes south. Your Emergency Alert Team.'

"Thanks for looking through the EAS website. We hope you know a little bit more about the team of EAS professionals who will be there for you, providing a soothing, helpful radio voice on December 21st, 2012, when life as we know it comes to an end. They are eager to go to work, but they understand it will take the greatest disaster in history to get them on the air. Once Armageddon is upon us, the EAS website will similarly swing into action. Why not bookmark it right now so that it's at your fingertips whenever the conflagration begins? With all hell breaking loose outside your window, you'll find the EAS website simple and easy to navigate. It also includes a comment board, where we welcome your feedback on our broadcast of the end of life as we know it. Sincerely, the team at EAS."

Points to ponder from the chapter "Bearers Of Bad Tidings"

As I write this, the Conservative government in Ottawa is attempting to reduce Canada's deficit by closing down departments and firing thousands of civil servants. There are rumours making the rounds in Ottawa that the Emergency Alert System might be on the list of cuts. An anonymous source close to a nameless high-ranking civil servant in the office of an undisclosed minister who asked that his name not be revealed for fear of recrimination by an unidentified source close to the PMO told me that the current thinking in the Prime Minister's office is that when the world ends, it might be more cost effective for the government, if a private radio station got the contract for alerting Canadians to the impending calamity. This normally would be done through an open bidding process, but, much like with the new fighter jets, the Prime Minister is taking a pass on the usual democratic process. Word on the street in Ottawa is that his favourite radio station, "99.2 The Canal" is close to being quietly awarded the contract, and on the day the earth explodes, all Canadians will get to hear their "Nice mix of soft hits and yesterday's favourites." There's also a rumour that the Prime Minister will appear "live" that day to play a few Beatles songs on the piano, but you never heard this from me.

When John regained consciousness moments after the earth had been blasted on December 21st, he found himself sitting in a beach chair amongst a pile of rubble. He and a dog named Gary were the only survivors. Despite many attempts by John, it appeared that Gary spoke no English.

8.

The Ten Safest Places In Canada To Wait Out The Apocalypse

#1. The Diefenbunker in Carp, Ontario

It's the perennial winner in the category of "Best Place to Survive the End of the World" in Ottawa's prestigious *Visitors' and Illegal Refugees' Guide to Ottawa* magazine. The Diefenbunker, or, more correctly, the Diefenbunker Cold War Museum, is easy to find. Let's say you were heading west out of Ottawa on Highway 417 to go to an Ottawa Senators hockey game at the Corel Centre and you had this sudden thought, "Do I really want to watch the Senators play tonight?", which happens a lot these days. Well, if you keep going a few hundred metres past the Corel Centre and turn right at Exit 144, you'll soon be in the aptly-named town of Carp, and that's where you'll find the Diefenbunker.

It's 100,000 square feet of blast-proof protection on four floors, all underground. It was originally built during the Cold War as the place where the Canadian Prime Minister, John Diefenbaker, could hide out while Russian missiles rained down nuclear holocaust, killing every other Canadian except him, his little dog, the woman who massaged his jowls, and his three dieffenbachia plants which were named Lester, Bowles and Pearson. When the nuclear nightmare was over, John Diefenbaker would have been the only man left in Canada, meaning that to repopulate the country, women would have needed to have sex with John Diefenbaker...so maybe Canada wouldn't get repopulated after all. Anyway, the Diefenbunker would have totally protected Mr. Diefenbaker from any jowl-rattling blast.

These days, deep down in the bowels of the bunker, under picturesque Carp, you can take a tour where you'll see the Prime Minister's suite, including the Diefenbunkbed where Diefenbaker would have Diefendropped off to sleep after a hard day of Diefenbroadcasting his message of hope to dead Canadians everywhere. There's a gift shop filled with memoraDiefenbelia, the War Cabinet room, plus the CBC Radio studio where a lonely CBC announcer would turn on his microphone once an hour and say, "At the beginning of the long dash, marking ten seconds of silence, it will be one o'clock Eastern Standard Time." They had to include the national time signal in the Diefenbunker, because this was the most popular radio broadcast in all of Canada during the 1960s. Canadians would drop what they were doing at the top of every hour and rush to the nearest radio to hear that reassuring time announcement. In the evening, families would gather round their radios to listen to the dulcet tones of the CBC announcer broadcasting the exact time, and that was one of the quirky things about Canadians back then. No approximate time would do. It had to be the exact time, "Geez, Bill, the village has been flattened by the A-bomb, you wouldn't happen to have the exact time, eh?"

But, back to the point, the first choice for all Canadians to totally protect themselves from whatever happens on December 21st should be the solid-as-a-rock Diefenbunker. So, here's how you can use the power of the mighty Diefenbunker to protect you when the Mayan Calendar runs out. Right now, before anyone else thinks of it, I want you to send an email to the Diefenbunker Museum and tell them you want to book a party of twenty (or however many people you want to save) on December 21st (Don't worry, they're open every day except Christmas, Easter, and New Year's Day, and December 21st falls on a Friday in 2012). You'll have to use subterfuge here. Tell them you want the tour to start at exactly six a.m. because your party has a busy schedule and needs to start early enough so they still have time to take in other great Ottawa area attractions, like longboard surfing at the Kanata Leisure Centre and Wave Pool, or the two o'clock Boa Constrictor feeding at

Little Ray's Reptile Zoo. The good folks at the Diefenbunker, now with visions of a big tip coming from your tour group, will happily accommodate you. Your real reason for the six a.m. start, of course, is that the Mayan Calendar ends at 11:11 a.m. UTC/GMT, which is five hours ahead of Ottawa. That means you'll be safely inside the blast doors and pretending to enjoy a tour of the Diefenbathroom when the world will end, and whether it's earthquakes, floods, swarms of flies, a plague of boils, or nuclear explosions, you and your tour guide will be chortling away about how fortunate you were to have been here, of all places, when it happened.

Make that call right now and book your fake Diefenbunker tour at 1-800-409-1965. Oh, yeah, and you'll see me there too, that morning, doing my own self-guided tour of the Diefenbarbeque pit. Wink, wink, nudge, nudge.

#2. The Hudson Bay Mining and Smelting facility in Northern Manitoba

You'll find this smelter located just off Route 10 in Flin Flon, past the sign that says, "Welcome to Flin Flon, Home of the scenic Precambrian Volcanic Belt." The smelter is easy to spot, just a few yards up the road from the Bobby Clarke statue with the iconic toothless smile—but watch out, if you come too close, the statue can whack you on the ankle with its hockey stick.

Once on the Hudson Bay Mining property, you should head for the abandoned copper mining tunnels deep underground. It was there from 2001 to 2009, a Saskatoon company grew medical marijuana for the Canadian government. This is a great place to sit through the end of the world, firstly because it's deep underground in tough-as-nails ancient basalt rock, and secondly, there may be a number of marijuana plants still lying around in the tunnels, which means you would be able to giggle your whole way through the end of the world. Don't forget to pack a lot of chips and dip. Totally!

#3. The Fairy Hole in Cape Breton, Nova Scotia

I know some of you would be reluctant to tell your loved ones that the world is ending and you're going into the Fairy Hole, but trust me, you'll be the one laughing when the all-clear has sounded. This cave is on Dauphin Bay on Cape Breton, and don't be put off by the fact that it's a sea cave and you're trying to save yourself from the potential world flood. This cave is sacred to the ancient Mi'kmaq people whose legend says that their hero Gluscap was last seen here before he disappeared into the hole and left the Earth world behind. Gluscap, obviously, knew what was at the end of the Fairy Hole and I'm guessing it's a place where you're safe from the troubles of the world. Who knows, you might find Gluscap still down there, along with Amelia Earhart, Jimmy Hoffa, and D.B. Cooper.

#4. The Roundhouse Lodge on Whistler Mountain, British Columbia

Easy to get to on the Whistler Village Gondola. Remember, Whistler is eight hours ahead of UTC/GMT, so you'll need to head up there the night before and hide under a counter, because nobody's supposed to stay there overnight. But it will be worth it, because if you want to escape the carnage on the ground or the seas *and* have a spectacular view of the Apocalypse, then you'll want to be 6,069 feet above ground. Besides being safe and sound on top of a magnificent pile of ancient metamorphic rock, the Roundhouse cafeteria is renowned for its steamed dumplings in a light miso broth. You could do a lot worse while the planet is exploding.

#5. The Lower Queen Subway Station in Toronto, Ontario

How to get there? Well, that's part of why this is such a good place to ride out the cataclysm. The Lower Queen station was only partially built but never used. It's way down underneath the Queen Street Station, and to get to it, you need to find your way through a locked door leading off the pedestrian underpass beneath the subway tracks. People who have seen it say it is dark and spooky, and they also say a scene from *A Nightmare on Elm Street* was filmed there, but I wouldn't worry about that because you'll be safe and sound, far below the "Nightmare on Queen Street."

#6. The Tunnels of Moose Jaw, Saskatchewan

If the idea of heading for cover in a Fairy Hole seems a little unmanly for you, try heading for cover in a Moose Jaw. There are tunnels running under the streets of Moose Jaw that were built in the early 1900s. They say that, in the 1920s, the tunnels were used by Al Capone and his Chicago gangsters to ship illegal booze during prohibition. This is not shocking to the people of Saskatchewan, where, at any given time, the jails are filled to overflowing with Conservative politicians. Anyway, this is probably a pretty safe place to hole up during the end of the world. Just head for downtown Moose Jaw, flip up a manhole cover and head down into the tunnels. Maybe, much like in Flin Flon, you might find a few bottles of Al Capone's whisky lying around the tunnels to help you forget.

#7. La Ville Souterraine in Montreal, Quebec

This hideout from the apocalypse will actually hold thousands of people, because Montreal is the most famous underground city in the world. It's true! Miles of underground cafés with hundreds of places to buy poutine. While Montrealers will be safe and sound down in their ville souterraine during the end of the world, they'll all be hoping that when they finally get back above ground, Quebec will actually have physically separated from Canada. Thank God, no more stupid referendums!

#8. Canada's fleet of submarines

Yes, there's an idea. What could be safer in a world-ending upheaval than being inside a submarine under the sea? Canada has one submarine stationed in Esquimalt and three submarines stationed in Halifax. The four submarines, all named after the giants of Canadian history, are HMCS Riel, HMCS Mulroney, HMCS Gretzky, and HMCS Bieber. I'm afraid you won't be able to just sneak onto the subs on December 21st, 2012, though. You'll have to join the Canadian Navy and ask for submarine duty, so better hop to it if you want to be safe when the Mayan Calendar runs out. And don't forget, Canada's submarines perform a very import role. I just wish I knew what it was.

#9. The town of Caledon, Ontario

You should move there immediately. Why, you might ask, would Caledon be the place to go when the world is falling apart? I'll tell you why. *Maclean's* magazine named Caledon the safest town in Canada, which means you're not going to get earthquakes there, or floods, or swarms of locusts, or any of the possible horrors that will happen once the Mayan Calendar ends on December 21st. Not in Canada's safest town. Also, you know you can completely trust *Maclean's* magazine. They have never been wrong yet choosing Canada's best university, have they? Besides, members of the Eaton Family, film director Norman Jewison, Shania Twain, and Elton John all own huge tracts of land in Caledon. These are all brilliant superstar thinkers who realized that *Maclean's* magazine was bang on and poured all their savings into Caledon, knowing full well that while catastrophes strike Mississauga, Ajax, and especially Etobicoke, the people of Caledon will be relaxing with a glass of Chardonnay and listening to "Candle in the Wind."

#10. Sussex, New Brunswick

You may know it better from its evocative motto "Gateway to the Fundy Experience." It's not that Sussex is a safe place to be during the end of the world, but Sussex is home to Atlantic Canada's largest hot-air balloon festival. I think you're catching my drift here. Now, December 21st isn't exactly ballooning season in New Brunswick, but in Sussex you'll find a lot of balloons stored in U-Haul lockers. A quick pop with a crowbar and they are yours for the taking. Fire up that propane burner, and you'll soon be drifting high into the sky, far above the maelstrom happening below and, unlike with airplanes, you won't have to come down until it's over, assuming you've stocked up on food and extra propane, and are adult enough to know that relieving yourself over the side of the basket at five thousand feet will not harm anyone on the ground. They'll have far more important things on their mind than a yellow shower.

So, there you are, a good selection of the safest places to head for in Canada when the Mayans destroy our world on December 21st, 2012.

Points to ponder from the chapter "The Ten Safest Places In Canada To Wait Out The Apocalypse"

I realize that many of you won't live anywhere near the ten places I've mentioned here, so when Armageddon strikes, what should you do? Right now you should Google the mayor of your city or town and find out where he or she will go in an emergency. They all have safe places, because when the world is ending, Canadians want to save their politicians first in order to carry on our wonderful way of life afterwards. Figure out the quickest route to get yourself to that safe place, and when the conflagration begins and they are asking for ID as local politicians are filing into their bunker, tell them that you are a pollster. I guarantee you they'll let you in, because politicians can get along without food or water for a week, but they can't live for a day without looking at polls. On the way to join your mayor, I recommend you protect yourself against falling things, or blowing things, by wearing a genuine BMX racers' helmet. Canadian Tire has one called the Kranked Halo Full Face Helmet, which features "a high-density fibreglass shell, EPS foam and new shape which combine for better protection in big falls, only $49.95 plus earn free Canadian Tire Dollars." I can't think of better protection in the face of whatever the Mayan Calendar throws our way.

Sensing that their home may be blown to bits when the world ends, Bill and Bart try to get used to living in a field.

9.

The Countdown

The precise end of the Mayan Calendar comes at 11:11 a.m. UTC/GMT. On Canada's East Coast, that's 6:11 a.m., and on Canada's West Coast that's 2:11 a.m. I doubt if anyone will want to go to sleep the night before. It'll be like Christmas when you were a kid, except that it won't be Santa's butt coming down your chimney—it'll be Halley's Comet. Now, if you like, you can wait for the end to come sitting in a corner and whimpering like the loser of a chair fight on Jerry Springer, or you can take it like a man or a woman and party like it's 1999! Now's the time to get that cocktail shaker out and whip up those Flaming Lamborghinis you've always wanted to pour down your throat (I would advise recovering alcoholics to stick to Near Beer or Virgin Shirley Temples on the miniscule, absolutely outside chance that nothing will happen when the Mayan Calendar runs out except that you've taken a nasty fall off the wagon).

Assuming you've taken one of the anti-death measures we've covered in other chapters, then you've got yourself covered as best you can. However, there will be people who will ignore all the tips I've given in this book and just stay where they are, becoming "The Man Who Laughed at Death." I don't really advise this unless you've tried it out before, such as being "The Man Who Laughed at Hells Angels" or "The Man Who Laughed at Doberman Pinschers." If you've done that and survived, then, sure, go ahead and start yukking it up when the Mayan Calendar ends. Regardless of where you are, though, this is the night to whoop it up like never before. I mean it's a once-in-a-lifetime event that may never come again, so go for the gusto.

Now then, who do you invite to this party to end all parties, this countdown to Armageddon? You should, at the very least, surround yourself with people you like. Forget about inviting the boss and sucking up to him for a raise or promotion to Vice President of General Awareness. I mean, the world is likely to end tonight and there may not be an office to go to tomorrow. Chances are the boss wouldn't be available anyway because he'll be attending his own end-of-the-world party with other people in his pay scale where they'll be toasting the Apocalypse as "the easiest set of layoffs they've ever pulled off." No, you'll want to be surrounded only by people you like. Generally, this won't include ex-husbands, ex-neighbours who used to let their dog take massive dumps on your lawn, or former chiropractors who tried to sell you a magnetic mattress while you were face down on his table and he had both hands on your neck (not that this ever happened to me). The same rule should apply to immediate family members, like that cousin from out west who drives a gigantic pickup truck that requires a stepladder to get into the cab, a shotgun rack in the back window, and a bumper sticker that says, "Let's go lynch some liberals!" He might be related by blood but when the countdown is on, he'll probably prefer to be standing, aiming his Remington 870 Wingmaster at the sky, yelling "Come and get me, you alien bastards!" Don't invite people who talk too much or talk too little, or have body odour issues, or who know all the words to any song by Grand Funk Railroad. Choose people you like. Call them up right now and tell them to come over on December 21st and bring a toothbrush, because, you never know, it might be a long sleepover.

Question: How should I dress for this end-of-the-world party?

Answer: You should dress to the nines! Men should rent the most expensive tuxedo they can find—after all, they might never have to take it back. Encourage your apocalypse guests to go all-out and look like they're in the ballroom scene from *The Shining*. If you have male friends who are Scottish, or even know anyone who is Scottish, invite them to wear a kilt. If it's their first (and, perhaps last) time wearing a kilt, they'll be elated with the incredible freedom of a kilt, allowing fresh air to circulate effortlessly around their genitals, inspiring them to belt out Scottish favourites like "Donald, Where's Your Trousers?" Encourage them to let their boys swing free and happy one last time. Women should wear party dresses that emphasize their best parts, especially their cleavage. Urge them to approach male guests and live out their fantasies of shimmying and shaking and doing lap-dance passes over the knee of their husband's best friend. This is no time to be timid, girls, and the bonus is: there may not be a morning after filled with guilt.

Question: Are there good party games everyone can play on the eve of destruction?

Answer: There are lots of party games, but none that are really appropriate for the cataclysm that may soon follow. I would stick to dancing and telling jokes. Dig out all the old sixties dance songs like "The Locomotion," "The Twist," and "The Hand Jive." They were all ridiculous dances, but trying to do them will take everyone's mind off the massive tragedy that is about to befall the planet. Is there any doubt which would be the best way to go out when the Hell Fires sweep you up: being a pouting wallflower, or flailing your arms in the air to "YMCA"? As to telling jokes, make an effort to remember the most profane jokes you have ever heard and shout them out lustily. Anything with guys walking into bars, prostitutes with wooden eyeballs, men with baby elephants' trunks transplanted in place of their penises, or even the hundreds of "Said the bishop to the actress" jokes that never fail to bring hearty chuckles. Laugh hard at all of them. If you are going to die a disgustingly painful death, why not do it with beer blowing out your nose?

That is option Number One for going through the countdown to the end of life. Option Number Two is watching it unfold on TV. Just because you haven't seen promos for it yet, doesn't mean that ABC won't be featuring Ryan Seacrest hosting *Rockin' Eve of Destruction*. According to Hollywood insiders, it's already in the works. They have booked Times Square where the giant "Ball of Destruction" will fall as we count down to the end of the Mayan Calendar. I have been assured that Dick Clark will participate in the countdown as the giant ball falls at 06:11 a.m. EST in Times Square. I've even been emailed a leaked copy of the script that Dick Clark will read as the crowds cheer and the great cataclysm nears. He will say, "Sorly donger buns deftaplate and dow arlen bestitude, Din! Noon! Eet! Suffen! Sex! Feist! Fur! Fleas! Dew! Wonk! Hoppy basgapfilderboon!" I've been told he's already practicing. So, yes, there should be lots of TV coverage if you choose to just sit on your couch and let life end with a soda in one hand and a bag of Oreos in the other. Just remember this: when we are all blown to bits on December 21st, even couch potatoes will have to die.

Points to ponder from the chapter "The Countdown"

I'll let you in on my fantasy scenario: how, if I could choose, I would spend the last few hours before Doomsday strikes. I would like to be in the front row at Royal Albert Hall in London for the Last Night of the Proms, standing straight in my tuxedo and Union Jack hat, belting out "Rule Britannia" as loud as I possibly could, and I'd be sure to hang on to my ticket stub because this, truly, would be the "Last" Night of the Proms. Do you have a fantasy Doomsday place? Does it involve Ukrainian sausages, or Chippendale male dancers? What about swimming naked with Angelina Jolie? Best of luck.

10.

How To Build Your Own Government And Get It Right This Time

On December 21st, 2012, the world will end and once the conflagration has cooled down you will notice that not only has much of humankind been wiped out, but many other species as well. In an eerie prediction written for its regularly scheduled CBC television program *Political Hinterland Who's Who*, you can hear the narrator saying,

> "As the fires of Armageddon begin to cool, the Political Hinterland has become a wasted landscape. Along the charred cliffs of the Rideau River, many creatures have become extinct. Nowhere can be seen any trace of the Weasel-Eyed Harper, or as it was known in

With the world about to end and nothing left to lose, Norman decided to let his best pal Rufus have his way with him.

Latin, dictatorus non transparentus. Look around you. Can you still spot the Snapping Baird, which was known by its Latin name, vicious ad canine-similarita? As the head of the orange wave, the Recanting Turmel, or in Latin socialista cum lately, has disappeared from the hills and valleys of Quebec along with her odd flock, known by their Latin name, boneheads grandiflora. Missing completely are the creatures of the upperchambers, the Senatorial Flock, in Latin, non-vital old farticus. All gone. No more will we see creatures such as the Silver-Headed Rae, its Latin name fresh facia same old ganglia. The Block Flock, known also by their Latin name sovereigntus irreleventitus, have been wiped out, although their extinction came earlier, allowing the other creatures to finally see the Block Flock off. The Mayan Calendar has ended, and in its fury, has wiped out the creatures of the Political Hinterland."

It's obvious that some old CBC programs were still the best, weren't they? So, you survey the mangled, post-apocalyptic countryside around you as one of the survivors of the Mayan Horror, and you think, "Well, it's over." But you would be wrong. In fact, this is the greatest political opportunity ever seen in Canada. The weary survivors of the Apocalypse need to be governed, but who is doing that? What are the other survivors doing? Foraging for food, going through dead people's wallets, stealing cars, looting DVD stores for copies of *Mad*

Men Season Five. Anarchy has set in. This, then, is the chance of a lifetime to fix things, to finally get it right. This is the time, and you are the person, to start the best government Canadians have ever seen. Please take your pencil now and begin underlining sentences in this section of the book and add as many notes in the margin as are required, because I am about to give you the blueprint for the perfect government.

First, you will need a sovereign territory, the land that you will govern. Because the mapping has already been done, I suggest claiming the original Canadian territory and I would stick with the name "Canada." I know there would be a temptation to change the name to something more appropriate like "Hockeyvakia," or "Beaverstan." Keep the name "Canada" and save money. There'll still be some old government stationery lying around you could use—I mean from before 2011, when "Canadian Government" was replaced on the stationery by the words "Harper Government." I know there will also be a temptation to get rid of certain parts of Canada that don't seem to be of much use, like Northern Saskatchewan, Labrador, or the corner of Steeles Avenue and Dufferin in Toronto. Yes, they're all crappy places, but they're part of the charm of Canada. And, whatever you do, don't get rid of anything north of sixty. Sure, it's cold and barren up there, but all those claims to the North Pole you've been hearing about will continue on in a post-apocalyptic world. Besides, one possible scenario that could happen on December 21st, 2012, is that the poles will shift, making Yellowknife the new Palm Springs, and wouldn't we want that as a selling feature of the new Canada? Imagine lounging by the pool at the Hay River Hyatt and Casino while the folks back home in Maui shovel their driveways. It could happen, so keep every part of Canada.

Okay, you've got a sovereign territory. Next, you will need to declare that you are an independent country. This is, mostly, just to stop people in what's left of the United States from taking us over. It's not that they are really interested in acquiring places like Regina or Hamilton (although they are pretty tempting); they just want our water and oil. So you draw up a declaration of independence and send it around to anybody who's left.

The third step will be to decide on what type of government you want, and here's where it's completely wide open, because you're starting from scratch. For example, you could choose an authoritarian style of government, which is a political system controlled by rulers who usually permit some degree of individual freedom, but then, that's what Canada had in 2012 so maybe you'd like to try something different. You could choose to set up a theocracy, which is rule by a religious elite, but...then again, that's what Canada had in 2012. If you were feeling in a really wacky mood, you could create a government like they had in the Land of Oz where a man hidden behind a curtain ran everything secretly, or... yeah, I know...what Canada had in 2012. I'm going to make a suggestion that might surprise you, but let me explain. Because you get to start any kind of government you want in the new Canada, you should choose only the best form of government ever invented, and that would be enlightened absolutism, which is a form of absolute monarchy, or despotism, in which the ruler is influenced by the Enlightenment, enlightenment being something the government didn't have in Canada in 2012.

So you declare yourself the absolute ruler, and just to reassure the citizens, you quote from Frederick the Great of Prussia, one of the leading proponents of enlightened absolutism, who said, "My principal occupation is to combat ignorance and prejudice...to enlighten minds, cultivate morality, and to make people as happy as it suits human nature, and as the means at my disposal permit." How about that? Isn't that something we've all been looking for in a government? No jingoistic political parties, no juvenile Question Period rants or overpaid, lazy senators, and, especially, no more wasting time having to read election material to decide whether to vote for a former realtor or a woman who worked as a bartender. I believe Frederick the Great was on to something with this enlightened absolutism. In fact, why don't you just call yourself Frederick the Great, even if your real name is Harvey or Sylvia. If a country is going to have an absolute ruler, then the ruler's name should have the word "great" in it somewhere.

Let's move on to the next step: a flag and a coat of arms for your country. First, the flag. Don't assume every Canadian loves the current flag. When Prime Minister Lester Pearson tried to introduce it in 1964, it started a debate that lasted six months and had people yelling at each other. It was not pretty. So, because you are now Frederick the Great of Canada, you can choose a new flag. Remember the great rush to be an English colony again that was all the rage before the Apocalypse? You know, putting "Royal" back in front of everything, like the Royal Canadian Navy or the Royal Canadian Air Force, or even the prime minister, who would have become the Royal Pain in the Ass? Forget it. England will be finished after doomsday, the royal family will be hiding out on Richard Branson's yacht and hooligans will control the streets of London, much like today. We can't be a colony of England if there is no England, can we?

Anyway, we'll need a new flag, and to really make Canadians cheer, you should do what should have been done years ago. Put a giant beaver on the flag. A beaver is neutral. He is neither French nor English. He lives everywhere in Canada. To give the flag some dignity, put a Mountie hat on the beaver and a hockey stick in one paw. Finally! The flag that says exactly what we are. Frederick, your subjects will be deliriously happy. For the coat of arms, you can do what you like, but if it were me, I would go with the same beaver from the flag gripping a snow shovel, while on the other side of the snow shovel is an obese man eating a donut. They are both standing on a banner with the new motto of your Canada. It says, in Latin, "*damnare suus dexteram frigida*," which in English translates as "Damn right it's cold!"

Last but not least, you will need citizens to fill the country.

Let's assume there are still a few dazed folks in Canada staggering around and coughing after the cataclysm has finished, but you'll need to entice more survivors from around the world to come to the new Canada. Run ads in any of the newspapers still left. The ads should say, "Come to Canada. Formerly the best country in the world. Now the only country in the world." You will need to fast track these immigrants so you can get the economy going in Canada, so the only question they will need to answer on their citizenship test should be "Who are you?" Accept anyone who gets over fifty per cent. And voila, you are ready to start running your country. It will need roads and buildings, bridges and schools, so you'll need to start levying taxes. Your subjects won't like it, but you'll just remind them, "I may be enlightened, but I am still a despot." Congratulations! You've just started your own government out of the ashes of the Mayan Calendar annihilation. Now, let's put a bid in for the next Olympics.

Points to Ponder from the chapter "How To Build Your Own Government and Get It Right This Time."

Naturally, there will be readers who will be offended that I've spent all this space ragging on Stephen Harper and his shifty ways. Let me say to you that you are wrong if you think I don't believe he is a top-notch leader. If you took world leaders such as Kim Jong Il, Muammar Gaddafi, Bashar Assad, Robert Mugabe, Mahmoud Ahmadinejad, or Hugo Chavez, and stuck them in a room, well, Stephen Harper is head and shoulders above all of them. I think I've made my point.

The Penguins waited until the Mayan Calendar officially ended before beginning their takeover of the earth. Minutes later, they sent columns of their troops out to round up humans.

11.
Excellent Business Opportunities After Doomsday

Let's begin this chapter with a short list of business ventures you shouldn't contemplate if you gain consciousness just after the crack of doom on December 21st, 2012 and begin thinking about things you could do. These businesses will be low on everyone's list after they have just survived the end of the world: nail salons, adult video stores, dude ranches, upholstery cleaners, dinner theatres, cat groomers, singing telegram deliveries, balloon artists, fortune cookie writers, dolphin trainers, fountain pen repair shops, perfume testers, rodeo clowns, cheese makers, cruise directors, faith healers, film critics, fortune tellers, image consultants, lottery ticket vendors, piano tuners, hockey referees, and lion tamers. Write this list on your hand so that, even if all your clothes have been blown off and there are no books or Post-it Notes available, you'll be able to quickly look into your hand, just like Sarah Palin does when she's speaking, and instantly know which business ventures you shouldn't undertake in a post-apocalyptic world.

Now, let's turn to the real moneymakers to turn you into an instant millionaire once the doomsday dust has settled. More than anything else, being in charge of all the money will make you richest the fastest. Obviously, the world has ended and so, too, the Canadian Mint, and I mean the one that churns out cash, not those sterling silver US military dog tags from the Tony Orlando Collection. That's the Franklin Mint you're thinking of, although I'm sure that, after Armageddon has blown over, you'll be able to trade those coins for things—maybe potatoes.

So the Canadian Mint is gone, what do you do? You start your own currency. Look around you. The countryside is littered with the wrecks of cars and that's where your new currency is. I want you to take the time to look inside the glove compartments of every one of those battered cars and, I guarantee, if they're anything like my car, you'll find Canadian Tire money stuffed in there. Take all of it. Put it away in a safe place. If you're not familiar with Canadian Tire money, here are the denominations: 5¢, 10¢, 25¢, 50¢, $1, and $2. These bills cannot be counterfeited because when the Bank of Canadian Tire made them, instead of using a picture of Queen

Elizabeth on the front, they chose the owner of Canadian Tire, and the man it was named after, Sandy McTire, a jolly Scotsman with a waxed moustache and beard, wearing a Tam O' Shanter with the Canadian Tire Hunting Tartan on it. The real Sandy McTire kept the master wooden printing block in a locked drawer. No doubt when the apocalypse hit, it would have been lost, along with Sandy's always-present bottle of eighteen-year-old Bowmore whisky.

Alright, that's the first step done: you now control all the money in Canada. In order to become a filthy rich banker (or is that redundant?), you must begin lending that Canadian Tire money out as soon as possible. Find the first young couple you can as they're wandering around in a daze and tell them, with a small down payment, you can finance their first new lean-to. With only their rare O-Pee-Chee WHA hockey card collection as a down payment, you will lend them the rest at the BS Rate (Bank of Sandy Rate), a twenty-year fixed rate mortgage of eighteen per cent. For collateral, all they will need is to leave their children with you until the mortgage is paid off (leasing out children to childless couples will become your secondary business, also making you a tidy profit). With that, you give the young couple a shoebox filled with Canadian Tire money and send them on their way. Then light up your first cigar.

But perhaps banking isn't how you see yourself getting rich in the earthly afterlife. If you are creatively inclined, I have a surefire money-maker that I know no one will have thought of: become a voice impersonator. Now, up until 2012, this was a career very few got involved with. There were plenty of hallway impersonators who could do five seconds of Homer Simpson saying "D'oh!," but the professional impersonators were few and far between. It was a hazardous business to get into. You could get paid a measly few hundred dollars (out of which your greedy slackass agent snapped up the first thirty per cent) and then put on a dazzling display of Barack Obama, Stephen Harper, Don Cherry, Marv Alberts, Jack Nicholson, Michael Caine, George W. Bush, and William Shatner impersonations, but, as impressive as that was, the audience, well and truly drunk by now, would start shouting out impossible requests: "Do Buster Keaton! Do Charlie Chaplin! Do Dick Clark!" And then all your "voices" eventually died or weren't re-elected.

Things will be different in the world after the end of time. A good impersonator will make a fortune because he or she will be able to impersonate anyone. Here's how: let's say there's a gang of semi-zombie thugs blocking everyone's way under an old overpass. You can do things to clear them out of the way. You can carry one of those giant ginsu-looking machete things that Denzel Washington had in *The Book of Eli* for hacking his way through a phalanx of semi-zombie thugs. The downside to that is that you have to be expertly trained in the use of that really dangerous weapon. The better way is using the powerful arsenal of a professional impersonator. You will have studied the zombie leader's voice for only a few minutes before you call out to his henchman, "Let the next guy through, the one with the shoeboxes full of Canadian Tire money. Nobody touches him or I will personally ram my shopping cart over their head." That's just one example of how being a professional impersonator can let you breeze through the wasteland that is earth without a scratch. You could impersonate entire villages of people voting to make you king. You will also be able to impersonate sheep, enough to make them come running, thinking it's feeding time before just bonking one over the head and cooking it that night on your campfire. Finally! It will have taken the destruction of the world for impersonators to get respect. I must warn you here. I'm only speaking about "voice" impersonators. If you have a talent as a female impersonator, I'm afraid this new world will be a dangerous place for a man trying to fight his way into Thunderdome looking like Liza Minnelli in six-inch stilettos.

And my last tip for running a successful business after the Mayan Calendar ends is such an obvious one. Create a new Mayan Calendar. You just need a chisel and an old stone grinding wheel from the wreckage of a gristmill. Hammer some little figures and numbers into the side of the wheel, make sure that some of the little figures have blowguns or spears or are carrying vases on their heads. In a few days, you'll have your new Mayan Calendar and you'll be ready to announce to everyone you see that you have found a new Mayan Calendar, not the Long Count. This one is the Short Count Calendar. Let them have a look at it and tell them only you can interpret the calendar...for a small fee. Then you will say this: "I will now explain how this Mayan Short Count Calendar works, which is similar to the Long Count Calendar. Rather than using a base-10 scheme, like western numbering, the Short Count days are tallied in a base-20 and base-18 scheme. Thus 0.0.0.1.5 is equal to twenty-five, and 0.0.0.2.0 is equal to forty. The Short Count is not consistently base-20, however, since the second digit from the right rolls over to zero when it reaches eighteen. Thus 0.0.1.0.0 does not represent four hundred days, but rather only three hundred and sixty days." When their eyes start to glaze over, have a small associate, a man with mousy hair and a limp, go through the crowd and pilfer as many pockets as possible. Clap your hands together to wake them up, and say, "What it means is that my Mayan Short Count Calendar will end on December 21st 2013, bringing on the end of the world, again, and I think it's the work of the Lord. If you are willing to listen to my weekly radio program and send me all the money you have, I will make sure you will accompany me on my journey to a heavenly reward when that awful day comes. Thank you friends."

I know many of you are saying, "Well, that method of making money is just criminal." It's not criminal. It's religion. It's just that sometimes religion seems the same as crime.

Anyway, there you have three surefire ways to make a fortune long after the annihilation has swept across planet Earth. While others are scrabbling, barehanded through rubble, and stripping copper plumbing out of houses, you'll have your feet up, counting your cash. Best of luck.

Points to Ponder from the chapter "Excellent Business Opportunities After Doomsday"

I honestly felt a bit creepy writing this chapter, because all these business opportunities in a post-apocalyptic world are based on greed, and I heard a lot of you saying to yourselves as you read this chapter, "But, Bob, what about those of us who just want to be bus drivers or librarians or blueberry farmers? What if we don't want to get rich on the scarred plains of planet Earth?" Well, as Bill Clinton once said, "I feel your pain...and your breasts are very nice, too." I'll be the first to admit that I can come up with great money-making ideas like I've listed in this chapter, but pulling them off is something I'm not great at. I'm not a great salesman. I'm with you people, so, after the great cataclysm has rolled across the world, I will be available to pick blueberries and maybe tell a few jokes as I'm picking them. It's not exactly multi-tasking, but there might be room in the new world for an amusing berry picker.

Believing they would survive the coming apocalypse by wearing their protective crowns, King Rudyard and his two queens began mapping out plans for their new kingdom.

12.

Questions From Frightened Readers

Judging from the hysteria now sweeping up every human on the planet over the date of December 21st, 2012, many people may still have many questions that have gone unanswered. I have tried to calm fears as much as possible by including some questions from readers on points about the massive cataclysm that I may have overlooked or edited out due to the overwhelming amount of material available on this touchy topic. I hope their questions will resonate with you, too.

First, a question from Charles "Chicken" Little from Upper Dildo, Newfoundland. He says, "Dear Bob, I've been running around for years now telling people that the sky is falling. It started when I was struck on the head by a falling acorn, and I was sure that was the beginning of the entire sky falling on me. Some of my friends like Frank "Foxy" Loxy and Kevin

"Cocky" Lockey think I'm right. Is it possible that the end of the Mayan Calendar signals that the sky is going to fall?"

Dear Charles,
Perhaps it might, but as with other scenarios, I believe it is definitely survivable. Being hit by a heavy falling object doesn't necessarily mean death. Let me quote you from a scientific paper written by Professor W. E. Coyote of the University of Arizona: "In one of our experiments I attempted to crawl out to the edge of a precipice in a futile attempt to capture a rare member of the *geococcyx californianus* family, the Greater Roadrunner. Unfortunately, the large tip of the cliff broke off, leaving me virtually running in mid-air and eventually plummeting to the ground, followed moments later by the massive piece of the cliff, which landed on top of me and flattened me to the shape of a pancake. Interestingly, it only took a few seconds to inflate back to my normal shape, and the only injury I suffered was an odd six-inch-high bump on my head, which made a strange whistling noise as it rose up." So, Charles, just because the sky could fall on you and your friends is no reason to fear it will kill you.

Next is a question from Styg Wiggins who lives in Head-Smashed-In Buffalo Jump, Alberta. He writes, "Dear Bob, You say that the Mayans are responsible for this calendar ending. Is Maya Angelou a Mayan and will she be partly responsible for the death of humankind?"

Dear Styg,

No, despite the name, she is not Mayan or related to the super race of Mayans. However, as that fateful date approaches you may want to read something that soothes your shattered nerves, and Maya has certainly written some thoughtful books. You'll find them all at your nearest New Age bookstore, along with other soothing titles like *Complete Chakra Alignment Plus Oil and Lube While You Wait*, or Paulo Coelho's latest offering in literary alchemy, *The Man Who Turned Kitty Litter Into Gold*. Styg, Maya Angelou is not someone to be afraid of. She actually might make your slow slide into purgatory a more peaceful passage. While I'm at it, let me also reassure you that John Mayall is also not a Mayan and, obviously, whatever happens on December 21st, 2012 will not be his fault, so there's no reason to turn your back on the blues and, certainly, no good reason to throw out your collectors' edition LP *Howlin' at the Moon*.

Our next reader question comes from Sheila P. Cox from Meat Cove, Nova Scotia, and she writes, "Dear Bob, I am generally considered a dimwit by my colleagues at the Nova Scotia School Book Depository, but I sense there's a surefire way to survive the coming apocalypse. The Mayans created this calendar. Surely, you would think that modern Mayans would be exempt from the fiery holocaust on December 21st, sort of like how Christians figure they will be exempt from the final showdown between good and evil all because they yelled out that they would take Jesus into their heart in order to save their ass on Judgment Day. Could this be true?"

Dear Sheila,
You may be a dimwit but you're on to something here. There have been whispered rumours over the past few years that built into the end of the Mayan Calendar program was a DNA exemption for anyone with Mayan blood, in other words, those whose blood is M-positive. And here is the loophole you were referring to in your question: go to the Yucatan Peninsula right now and get pregnant by a Mayan man. Believe me, modern-day Mayans are an attractive people so there'll be no problem falling for one. The problem may be, and I'm only guessing this, that annoying stammer and your unfortunate habit of passing gas at the most inopportune times has made you into someone who is not exactly hunk-bait. You can remedy this by wearing an extremely short skirt and, at every opportunity, climbing onto a table at the Cancun Coco Bongo and flashing your knickers to all men in the vicinity. This will, likely, lead to an invitation to a Mayan shack at the northern end of Kukulcan Boulevard, where they make the genuine Panama Hats in a cave under the shack. Perhaps his name will be Jesús...interesting! After a dozen Mojitos and a night of wild Mayan passion, including whips, marimbas and blue agave mashers, you will be close to your "Get Out of Hell" card. If you can give birth to Jesús's child, you immediately jump onto the "Apocalypse Exempt List" and

will not die on December 21st, 2012. To move even higher up the list, give that child a Mayan name, as opposed to the "Ethan" or "Olivia" that you were planning on. Instead, secure your place in the Mayan Afterlife by naming your child "Xochixquetzal" if it's a boy or "Yacatecuzhtli" if it's a girl. Believe me, all the Mayan gods, even Xipe Totec, will take note. Best of luck on your quest, Sheila!

Here's a question from Axel Bagger, who lives in Middelfart, Denmark. He writes, "Dear Bob, Should I treat the night of December 20th like I am a prisoner on Death Row and indulge myself with the greatest last meal ever?"

Dear Axel,
It might seem like the right thing to do, rustling up a heaping plate of bangers and mash or chicken-fried steak and cajun potato wedges, or even bean burritos with mexican rice and refried beans (I'm getting hungry just thinking about these), but you should, in fact, be preparing a light meal in preparation for your head-on meeting with oblivion. Normally, nutritionists would recommend fibre in a meal, but not this time, and here's why: on December 21st, when you run outside your house and see a four-hundred-foot-high tsunami wave coming down your street, you should be evacuating your family, not evacuating your bowels, and, believe me, the sight of a four-hundred-foot moving wall of water will blast open the external anal sphincter of any human being. That's when you'll

thank me for suggesting something light to eat, what I call my "Recipe for Disaster": half a grapefruit, followed by an egg whites omelet with half a lightly-buttered English muffin, accompanied by a steaming cup of green tea (loose, never tea bags). I recommend a little light exercise, perhaps twenty minutes of calisthenics which is vital, because if you have to run for your life from red hot magma or a swarm of flies with a large child or woman on your back, you'll need to be in good enough shape that you're not winded after the first fifty miles. Follow your exercise session with a refreshing shower and hold off on the perfumed soaps and shampoos. If you do indeed end up travelling to an afterlife, I doubt perfumes of any sort will be tolerated, and if you wake up after the almighty blast in a scene like something out of a *Mad Max* movie, then smelling like Jessica Simpson's "Fancy" will probably get you shot or eaten by a pack of wild dogs (I'm told that wild dogs go crazy after smelling Jessica Simpson's "Fancy").

This question comes from Scoop Turner, who writes from his home in Spuzzum, British Columbia, which is beyond Hope. Scoop says, "Dear Bob, In preparation for the end of the world, do you think I should start collecting pairs of animals?"

Dear Scoop,
If you intend to open a zoo once the conflagration has died down, then, sure, collecting pairs of animals would be a good idea, but the process is filled with many hazards, not least of

which is that you could die a grizzly death—that is, being ripped apart by a grizzly bear that does not welcome the idea of being rounded up. I would recommend that if you decide to do this, you should hire a zoologist and a veteran animal wrangler. The zoologist is important because if you can't tell the difference between a male sloth and a female sloth, for example, then you might accidentally collect two male sloths and you will be waiting a very long time for mating to begin, not that they might not come to like each other or even begin sharing a cuddle or two. The fact is that, due to your ignorance, you will have exterminated the sloth population. A zoologist will make sure this doesn't happen. The animal wrangler is equally important because, outside of koalas, pandas, and certain breeds of tortoises, most animals can kick up quite a fuss when you try to stuff them into a cage. Camels, for example, will kick or spit or both as you are trying to shove them into the back of a van. An animal wrangler is the only one who should do this kind of work, but even then, it's dangerous. I've seen numerous wranglers come on as guests on late night TV talk shows and be badly scratched by a rare Tunisian hyena, or nearly lose their manhood with a vicious peck from the beak of a giant Bolivian wild turkey. Be warned! It may have come naturally to Noah, but collecting pairs of wild animals is not for everyone. And remember, if the end of the world is a biblical-type of flood and you've built a boat big enough to hold your menagerie, then fine, but if, instead, it's an earthquake or firestorm, then all these pairs of animals will have to share your lean-to and, unless you want to be kept up all night by croaking cane toads and howling coyotes, I wouldn't do it. If you do decide to go ahead, one tip that'll make your work easier: don't try and get pairs of every creature on earth. I think after all this time, we can accept that there are some we'd rather do without. Mosquitoes, for example. Also, tapeworms, ostriches, slugs, cockapoos, maltipoos, any animal with the word "poo" in its name, and, of course, telemarketers.

Here's a question from Dick Orchard in Wetwang, Driffield, North Humberside, UK. He writes, "Dear Bob, Will my mobile phone still work after the world has ended?"

Dear Dick,
Don't be ridiculous! The world, as you say, will have ended, which means all thirty-five thousand mobile phone masts in the UK will be down. You'll need to find a landline.

The next question was sent from Harshit Singh Paliwal in Elbow, Saskatchewan. He writes, "Dear Bob, What's the best time zone to be in when Doomsday strikes on December 21st, 2012?"

Dear Harshit,
Good question. I would say anywhere in Scandinavia. They are in the Central European Time Zone, and because the

Mayan Calendar ends at 11:11 a.m. UTC, and will then roll westward, the people of Scandinavia will have twenty-three hours to observe and, hopefully, learn from what happens during the maelstrom.

Now I've got a question from Wanda Ho who lives in Saint-Louis-du-Ha! Ha!, Quebec. She writes, "Dear Bob, I read with interest your answer to Sheila P. Cox about securing an exemption from the gruesome death that will surely occur on December 21st by getting yourself pregnant by a Mayan man and having his baby. I love my husband, Hugh Ho, and could never have sex with another man, not after the way Hugh looks after the children and me and has worked so hard at building a successful wagon repair business, Wagons Ho, just off the Centreville Exit on Route 185. So, if I can't get pregnant by a Mayan, is there still a way to get the "Mayan Doomsday Exemption"?

Dear Wanda,
I was once told by an old Mayan woman I met, as she walked beside her donkey on the road to Chichicastenango, that there's a good chance you can obtain the "Mayan Doomsday Exemption" even if you are unable to give birth to a Mayan child. You could try adopting a Mayan family. For only a few dollars month, you'll help them build the well in their village, plus they'll send you photos of their family posing in front of the hacienda. If you can't adopt a family, you could adopt a highway. Apparently, Highway 186 to Rio Bec

has been orphaned for over twenty years. If none of the above is doable, try to befriend at least one Mayan person, or more if you're capable, and please note, according to the Long Count Calendar, joining a Mayan Facebook page doesn't count as making friends. In their prescient genius, the ancient Mayans understood that "meeting" on the Internet is not actually human interaction. They knew thousands of years before us that your new online friend might say she's just a simple Mayan milkmaid named Juanita, when, in fact, he is a one-eyed, toothless Slovakian criminal named Jaroslav. No, you'll need to meet Mayans face to face and there's a good reason, which I'll tell you in a second. I recommend you go down there and join the local Oxkutzcab Lions Club and make some friends, or just chat people up over coffee in a Cancun café. Here's why, according to the old lady on the road to Chichicastenango, you need to do this. Based on her reading of the Long Count, you will need to be touching a Mayan when 11:11 a.m. UTC rolls around. At the very least, get yourself down there, go to a market square, and seconds before the Apocalypse strikes, hold hands with someone. It might seem a little inappropriate, but, hey, it's only for a few seconds before you're both whisked away to the scorpion-filled rivers of Xibal. Ooh! That doesn't sound good. Maybe the old lady with the donkey was pulling my leg.

The final question I've chosen comes from Elmer Doidge who lives in Humptulips, Washington. He writes, "Dear Bob, I've read your book and followed most of your tips and I'm now ready for whatever the Mayan gods throw at me. But, I have a lingering worry. I hope you can reassure me. What happens, on December 21st, 2012 if the clock strikes 11:11 a.m. UTC and nothing happens?"

Dear Elmer,
Very quickly, and before anyone else thinks of it, you should get on Craigslist and sell that giant boat you built with food rations to last a year. Because it's Craigslist, the callers will try and grind you down, but you might get your money back. Hang on to that fully stocked, underground bunker you built in your back garden. Someday, the government will outlaw smoking in your own house, and you'll be the only one on your block with a secret place to go and light up. You'll have some phone calls to make: you'll need to get through to the cable company and tell them someone must have been impersonating you when they called to cancel the cable and said "and you guys are all assholes, too!" Show up at work and explain to the guy in the corner office that showing him the middle finger, like you did yesterday, is actually a sign of great respect in Namibia and you are...one eighth Namibian. You'll want to knock on the neighbour's door and tell him the note you left that said, "Oh, by the way, Dickhead, the pruning shears, the weed whacker, and the set of Callaway golf clubs that you took your bloody time returning? Well, keep 'em, pal! What part of 'borrowing' didn't you understand?" must have

come from the guy who lives in the other house. Most of all, husbands and wives must sit their other half down and say, "Okay, death, apparently, did not us part, but there's always tomorrow! After all, Pastor Harold Camping has his calculator out and there's bound to be another announcement soon."

13.

Mayan Horror Readers Book Club

DISCUSSION QUESTIONS

Of all the possible tragedies that humanity could suffer on December 21st, 2012, which is your favourite and why?

Count the number of times the author has used the words "apocalypse," "armageddon," and "cataclysm." Wonder aloud why he didn't use the word "badonkadonk" even once.

Why did the author ignore one of the more obvious horrific events to take place on doomsday: death by a thousand tiny pricks? Is this a veiled reference to oil company executives?

When Pope Gregory designed his calendar, he opted to have his calendar end once a year instead of once every 5126 years like the Mayans. Discuss whether this was to boost sales of his calendar as the perfect Christmas stocking stuffer.

We know that the man who designed the Mayan Calendar was named Xiuhtecuxhtzli, but can you name the other partners in his publishing company?

Open a discussion about how Buddhists will react when they are reincarnated after December 21st, 2012 and discover the earth is gone. Will they become uncharacteristically furious?

Get everyone to guess which major chain of retail stores will be the first to advertise a December 21st "Major Blow-Out Sale. Everyone Must Go!"

When the Emergency Alert System radio station kicks in on December 21st, will their format be Classic Rock, Alternative Album Contemporary, or a pleasant mix of Today's Hits and Yesterday's Favourites? Will they take requests, and will they do on-location broadcasts from smoking volcano craters?

Discuss why there has been so much emphasis on the Mayan Calendar, but very little talk about the Mayan Thesaurus or the Mayan Rhyming Dictionary.

Name the female politician on the front cover of the book and what she did to cause blood to shoot out of her eyes.

Mayan Horror Index

Aawk 345-346, a bird indigenous to Honduras, flightless with no feathers and no legs, a major part of the Mayan cuisine, especially the famous Aawk Pie, derives its name from the sound it makes when someone trips over it.

Akron 6-15, city in Ohio never visited by Mayans.

Arbitration 688, 704, method used to solve land disputes between Mayans and Aztecs.

Astrophysics 241-250, taught to the Mayans by alien beings from the Van Allen Belt, who also introduced the Mayans to belts and pocket puffs.

Auntie Phlegm 72-78, fortune teller at 34th and Vine, replaced Madame Ruth, you know, that gypsy with the gold-capped tooth selling little bottles of Love Potion #9.

Barbershop Quartet 69, 88, 96, featured entertainment at all Mayan Solstice festivals.

Bistackomelen 237-397, a word that has no meaning in the Mayan or English languages.

Bog 54-59, colloquial name for Mayan latrine, a deep pit dug in the nearby jungle. Used in Mayan conversation as in "I'll be in the bog if anyone needs me."

Buster 86-88, one of the lesser-known Mayan leaders, even though he was born Checuattlaxingzu, he preferred to be called "Buster," which caused him to be frequently overlooked when new chiefs were chosen.

Brains 3, 765, a delicacy for Mayan children following a ritual human sacrifice, wherein parts of a human body were passed around for consumption. Mayan mothers delighted their children when they yelled, "Who wants brains?"

Calendar 1-2012, a Mayan device for measuring the passage of time. Many different types of calendars were created by the Mayans and all of them ended with somebody getting hurt.

Catharsis 123, 321, a session of talking and purging bad feelings for Mayan priests who accidentally chose their mothers for human sacrifice.

Chichen Itza 47, 598, a large pre-Columbian site built by the Maya. Some archeologists think the name means "At the mouth of the well of the Itza" while others believe it is a combination of the Mayan words "Chichen," meaning "chicken" and "Itza," an early type of pizza, making the site the first fast food outlet in the Yucatan.

Chihuahua 965-967, a northern Mexican state often visited by the Mayans. Also a small animal eaten as a snack by Mayan children.

Chipotle Dip 879, 903, a sauce introduced by the Mayans made from smoke-dried jalapeño, perfect for dipping roasted weasel legs.

Cloaking Device 36-37, later adopted by scientists aboard the Starship Enterprise, in Mayan times it was simply a cloak for wearing on cool nights and was quite ineffective at protecting Mayans from Klingons.

Cretch 624, 762, a combination of coughing and wretching at the same time, invented by the Mayans after over-indulging in too many chili-pepper-and-breadnut sandwiches.

Cynthia 645, 899, revered as the largest Dasypodidae or Armadillo ever encountered by Mayan hunters, the animal with a repulsive smell weighed well over eighty pounds and was five feet in length, large enough for Mayan hunters to honour it by naming it Cynthia.

Day Timer 89-106, a miniature, pocket-sized version of the Mayan Calendar used by Mayan executives to keep track of the cost of their blowgun inventory.

Dead 621-643, the consequence for any Mayan who stepped into a rattlesnake nest.

Diego Estupido 57, 64, 79, also known as the dumbest of the Conquistadors, who tried to conquer the Mayans armed with only a small knife and a whip. Later became a filling in Mayan tacos.

"Don't Be Cruel" 385-387, an Elvis Presley song noted for containing no mention of Mayans.

Druamel 482, 566, a cigarette invented by the Mayans and introduced to the Spanish. Mayan smokers liked to say; "I'd walk a mile for a Druamel."

Ecuador 43-54, where Mayans went to escape the harsh winter temperatures of thirty degrees Celsius, especially the beach resorts of Salinas, which offered rooms at par for Mayans.

Eduary 56, 86, 104, in the Mayan Calendar, it was the third month out of thirteen on the yearly calendar, as in January, February, Eduary. The month was named after the Mayan inventor of whole-wheat tortillas, Eduary Estrada.

Eel 435, 577, a type of fish found in the Xantualepyx River, eaten frequently by Mayans, also used in a Mayan joke greeting, as in "Is that an eel in your breechcloth, or are you just happy to see me?"

Entertainer 690-765, comedy performers similar to jesters in medieval times, a Mayan leader who was feeling sad after losing a massive battle to the Toltecs would call for the court entertainer, called a yucatero, to cheer him up.

If the yucatero failed to make the leader laugh, he was hung from his funny bone until dead. Very few Mayans aspired to be entertainers.

Fart 209-210, foul gas being expelled by the body, worshipped by Mayans who believed it was Itzamna, the Reptile God who spoke through people's anuses.

Ferguson 577-580, a Scottish con man who landed in Honduras with Hernán Cortés' army, and tried to sell the Mayans a machine that turned corn into gold. Once they discovered it was a trick, he was chased out of town by angry Mayan warriors who soon caught up to him. He became known in Mayan legends as "Not-So-Fast Ferguson."

Fester 56-57, what happened to a wound made by a Mayan poison-tipped arrow.

Fondue 214, 306, a type of meal introduced to the Mayans by the only Swedish Conquistador, Lars Larson, but failed to catch on because Mayans didn't use cheese.

Futbal 89, 96, 105, a sport invented by Mayans where players used both their hands and feet and often dove to the pitch in contrived pain; a forerunner of modern soccer.

Gangrene 14-22, a necrosis of the skin on certain limbs of the body which Mayans avoided eating; children were often warned, "Don't eat the green feet!"

Geeks 565-568, a tiny portion of the Mayan population that actually understood the subatomic physics used to construct their temples, carried writing instruments in early pocket protectors.

Gird 967, 988, a method used by Mayans to cover their loins.

Gore 877-878, an American politician who not only invented the Internet, but also invented the Mayan Calendar.

Groper 456, 571, a fish eaten by Mayans, also the name used to describe elderly Mayan warriors who prepared the virgins for sacrifice.

Happy 79-85, a famous Mayan children's entertainer, simply known as Happy the Honduran Clown, put on shows at all Yucatan beach towns and did simple magic tricks. A favourite trick involved pulling an anteater out of a hat.

Harbinger 35-39, a negative word often used by Mayans to describe the moment Christopher Columbus stuck his flag in the sand at San Salvador.

Heads up! 447-456, a Mayan expression meaning, "Watch out for the jaguar jumping at you from the tree!"

Hirsute 65-68, used by Mayans to describe the bearded faces of the Spanish Conquistadors, also the upper lips of their elderly wives.

Hopi 99-103, an Indian tribe from Arizona and Mexico, related to the Mayans, did not create a world-ending calendar, but did make extensive use of greeting cards.

Ida Lupino 123-130, famous TV and film actress who appeared in a film called *The Bigamist* which, strangely enough, was what the Mayans called the early morning fog in the jungle.

Indigenous 456-457, a word meaning, "original owners of the land," well understood by the Mayans, not understood at all by the Spanish and Portuguese.

Jalapeño 911, 934, used in the rite-of-passage ceremony for all Mayan boys. The boys would become men if they sacked a Toltec village, wrestled a jaguar, and ate fifty jalapeños without getting the hiccups.

Jiminy! 39, 56, 78, 82, 99, a much-used Mayan expression, often yelled out after being gored in the groin by a warthog.

Jumping Bean 87-88, still sold as toys called Mexican Jumping Beans, they were invented by the Mayans as a source of amusement, along with other games, such as one that involved making captured Incas walk on hot coals, known as Jumping Men.

Knickers 65, 98, 73, underwear worn by Mayan women made from coconut shells, very scratchy to wear, resulting in most Mayan women abandoning underwear and going, as the Mayans called it, "Commando."

Landowners 654-655, how the Mayans introduced themselves to the Conquistadors, who misheard and thought the Mayans were saying, "Please kill most of us, take everything we've got, bring thousands more settlers, convert us to Christianity, and wipe out our civilization." What a difference a Mayan translator would have made!

Lope 89, 106, a fast method of running practiced by Mayan warriors who were being chased by a family of scorpions.

Mesquite 348, 401, a type of hard wood used by Mayans for barbecuing freshly caught Aztecs.

Moron 566-567, a Mayan word used to describe the King of Spain.

Nayam 34, 127, 385, a branch of the Mayan race also known as the "Backward Mayans," a breakaway tribe that lived in the hills outside Campeche. Cousins frequently married cousins; battles were fought over hidden stills of banana liquor. First known use of the banjo.

Nose Hairs, The 18-22, a popular Mayan rock group.

Obdiplostemonous 56-57, a term used by Mayans meaning a flower that had twice as many stamens as petals, the study of which was enjoyed by a tiny percentage of Mayan men called Obdiplostemoners, or Warriors of the Pansy.

Ornery 783, 841, a condition brought on when a Mayan steps on a colony of fire ants.

Pedometer 611, 733, an early method for Mayans to count how far they had walked. An Aztec slave would follow them through the jungle, yelling out "One! Two!" etc., at each step taken by the Mayan.

Prickly Pear Cactus 441, 552, a fruit eaten as dessert by the Mayans, also part of an old Mayan joke, "What is the difference between a ship full of Spaniards and a Prickly Pear Cactus?" (Answer: "With the cactus, the pricks are all on the outside.")

Quack 65, 105, 266, a Mayan practicing as a medicine man but without training in bloodletting or the proper insertion of porcupine quills.

Queen 188, a Mayan warrior with far too many bright feathers in his headdress.

Quiz 663-668, a regular feature of Trivia Night at a Mayan Pub, or as Mayans called them, "Quaffo i Pukez." A typical quiz question would be "What was the name of the alien spaceship that landed and taught us about mathematics?" (Answer: "Queen of the Galaxy.")

Quorum 89-94, the minimum number of members required to legally begin a monthly shareholders meeting of the Mayan Maize Board.

Ribald 277-279, the type of songs sung by Mayans round the temple bonfire, especially the popular sing-along, "Xecuetxzluan's in the Jungle with a Monkey."

Roquefort 776-778, a type of salad dressing used by Mayans, although not as popular as Mayanaise.

Ruin 123, 456, the remains of ancient Mayan sites, also the name used to describe an elderly Mayan who had chewed too many cacao leaves.

Sack 18, 45, 66, a much-used Mayan word with two meanings: to attack an Aztec village and plunder all their precious items, like Onyx keychains, lava rock ashtrays, and shark tooth necklaces; also a word to describe when employees of a Mayan temple were laid off due to a downsizing order from temple corporate headquarters in Uxmal.

Soup, 601-603, a main part of the Mayan diet; popular favourites were Spicy Termite Bisque and Hearty Iguana Stew, which most Mayans said tasted like chicken.

Tequila 306-309, a medicine made from blue agave plants, used by Mayan priests to treat people feeling very unhappy; all patients reported they quickly became very happy... with a strange urge to sing "La Cucaracha."

The Trots 127-130, a condition caused by making Montezuma angry.

Think yo 566-580, an expression of gratitude spoken by teenage Mayan girls.

Umbilical cord 389-391, the membranous duct connecting the fetus with the placenta; ancient Mayans did not cut off the umbilical cord at birth. It was left connected for five years so that Mayan mothers could keep their children from running off when they weren't looking.

Vacuum cleaner 137, 186, invented by the Mayans long before modern technology arrived; the Mayans would train anteaters to clean their carpets, sucking up everything on the floor, including hundreds of ants.

White-lipped peccary 76-78, a wild pig hunted by Mayans; because of its nutritional value, it was promoted by Mayan leaders in a campaign titled "Put some Peccary on your Fork."

Xentualopizicutlasuxochuchualentlox 58, 744, the longest known word in the Mayan language, pronounced "dork," often used by Mayan warriors to describe unpopular leaders.

Zoom zoom zoom 411-412, a Mayan blowgun capable of firing poison darts at a rate of several hundred rounds per minute, killing hundreds of enemy warriors, as well as the blowgun shooter, who died of exhaustion.

OTHER BOOKS BY BOB ROBERTSON

The Rise and Fall of the Roman Umpire
The previously untold story of Luigi Puzzolente, who rapidly rose to become the top umpire in the Italiana Softball League, but fell out of favour over time because he had no clearly defined strike zone, resulting in many inches-from-your-face arguments with players and managers. Being from Rome, Italy, Luigi's Penne Alioli breath caused such revulsion that he was banned from ever umpiring again, and he ended his days as a purse thief on the #64 Bus. The book was nominated for Italy's prestigious Remainders Prize.

The Proboscis of the Moon Snail
A frightening horror novel about a scientist who studies Moon Snails, or *naticidae*, and accidentally falls into the tank where the Moon Snails are kept, where he is attacked by a giant Moon Snail he has named "Bob." Bob uses his elongated proboscis to bore a hole into the scientist's head, suck out the brain and organs, and escape from his tank. Bob wreaks havoc on the world despite the fact that he moves very, very slowly. The book was the winner of the Frightful Books of 2008 Award.

1,000 Ridiculous Things to do Before You Die
Drawing on his own personal experiences as well as those of his friends, Bob Robertson gives you the ultimate bucket

list. Yes, you could travel to Spain and walk the El Camino, or you could swim with the stingrays in Bora Bora, but everybody does those things before they die. This book guides you down a different road, where you fill out the rest of your days doing things like taking a hair dryer into the shower, aiming a laser pointer into your eyes, walking into a Taliban camp singing "God Bless America," or starting an opposition party in China. There's tons of ideas in this book to help you not only do all these ridiculous things before you die, but actually die doing most of them. Listed by *Bum Packers International* as "a book to carry in your top pocket as you stroll through Mogadishu, because it will stop a bullet to the heart."

The Miracle Pencil Diet

Based on decades of anecdotal evidence, Bob Robertson's miracle diet is a discovery that could change the world. He tracked the lives of classmates who, he remembered, chewed on their pencils while in school, and those who didn't. The results were startling: those who chewed pencils appear to have gone on to lives as professionals such as doctors, lawyers, accountants, and physicists, while those who didn't chew pencils ended up at the losing end of life, as convenience store clerks, backhoe operators or, even worse, comedy writers. The result is obvious: spending your teenage years chewing on an HB yellow pencil, with its powerful combination of cedar, lead, and rubber, appears to incite the brain to greatness. Robertson recommends chewing a wooden pencil before every meal and even offers an online shop that will supply you with lead pencils the rest of your...exciting and fulfilling life. Go to ieatleadpencils.ca and order yours today. Readers of this review will automatically receive 50% off their first order.

ACKNOWLEDGEMENTS

This book would not have been possible without the help of Brian Kaufman and the hundreds of talented editors at Anvil Press. More than anything I am grateful to Brian for agreeing to publish this book even after realizing he had misheard me when I was pitching the idea, probably because of the loud party we were both at, the after-party following the annual Vancouver Water Main Flushing (Beaver Bollocks was the featured band so you can imagine how loud it really was). I'd had a few too many glasses of GlenSather so that didn't help. As I screamed my idea into Brian's ear, he thought I'd said "How about a book called *My Auntie Karen's Racy Calendar Photos*?" He nodded so hard I thought his head was going to fall off. So, even in the clear light of day the following morning at the JJ Bean Coffee Shop, when I told him what I'd really said, he still agreed to go ahead with the book. Publishers like Brian Kaufman are...well, now I'm starting to tear up. Thank you, Brian!

Also, this book could not have been written without the help of Professor A. Jinkerson, who very kindly wrote the introduction. Professor Jinkerson, or just plain "Adolf" as he prefers to be called, took a massive amount of time away from his Armageddon Lab at USBC to buy me coffee at many of Pitt Meadows' finest coffee shops, like The Pitts Coffee House and Katzie Slough's Coffee Dregs. In those coffee chats he enlightened me like no one else could on the variety of ways that humans could be destroyed. I listened like an enchanted child as he spoke of people being vaporized in a neutron firestorm seconds after bleeding profusely through their anus. While most others around the coffee shop were arguing about the Vancouver Canucks, Adolf and I were zeroing in on the really important stuff of life—gruesome human annihilation. For that, I will be eternally grateful.

I'd also like to thank the very kind tour guides at the Diefenbunker in Carp, Ontario, for their patience at my many questions about why John Diefenbaker got a bunker named after him and yet other Canadian prime ministers didn't. "What happened," I asked them, "to the Brian Bastion or Harper's Arsenal?" Regardless of my idiotic questions, they were extremely patient. I hope their employment there gets them to the head of the line on Judgment Day.

I would also like to thank the following people and organizations for their help in getting this book written: Barney Zack and the staff at Cyclone Mailers' Blow Gun Rentals, the folks at the Ah Puch Mayan Music Shop for introducing me to the modern music of the Mayans, especially the red hot Mayan rapper Pablo Ten Pesos. I have downloaded everything he has recorded from iTunes. Many thanks to Arlene Beamer and the women of the Medicine Hat Women's Glee Club, Jim Beam and Associates for constant inspiration, the Finn Slough Fire Brigade, the Harley S. McGillicutty Clog Dancers, the Spuzzum Clinic for the Criminally Insane, Nina's Napkins in

Nanaimo, Billy Becker, Doctor Dan, The Salt Spring Walnut Society, the Cooley Corners Grocery and Fireworks Superstore, Super Urologist Dick Trickle, Bev 'Beaver' Benson, Fizzy Gibson, the Ajax Corner Store and the Two Hills Perogie Farm. Thank you all!

ABOUT THE AUTHOR

Bob Robertson is a successful comedy writer in books and newspaper columns as well as co-creator and writer of the award-winning Canadian comedy series *Double Exposure* on CBC Radio and Television, CTV and The Comedy Network. He lives with his wife, Linda Cullen, in New Westminster, B.C.